THE FINVISOR'S MOJO

9 Lessons
for a Financial Advisor
to Build a Powerful Business

FROM AN INDUSTRY EXPERT

GARVIT CHAHARIA

notionpress.com

INDIA · SINGAPORE · MALAYSIA

Notion Press Media Pvt Ltd

No. 50, Chettiyar Agaram Main Road,
Vanagaram, Chennai, Tamil Nadu – 600 095

First Published by Notion Press 2021

ISBN 978-1-68523-458-4
HC: 979-8-89415-908-9

CONTENTS

ACKNOWLEDGEMENTS

Writing a book is a journey which cannot be carried out alone. A lot of people have helped me shape my thoughts into this book. I shall forever remain indebted to them.

THANK YOU!

Papa, for being my guardian angel and guiding me always. I miss you.

Maa, for everything.

Supriya, my wife, for being with me through thick and thin.

Mr Vinayak Sapre, author and speaker, for being the inspiration which led me to write this book. Your mentoring has helped me grow.

Mr Brijesh Dalmia, business coach, for guiding me through your words. A lot of business learning has come from you.

Rahul, for teaching me culture and ethics of insurance business. Your guidance has helped me significantly.

Mr Navneet Batra, for being a great friend. Your advice has broadened my vision about the industry.

BNI, for helping me change the way I do business.

My clients, for trusting me. Without your support I wouldn't have dared to dream this big.

Company folks, for being available always. Your guidance has been overwhelming.

My employees at Deeva Ventures for looking up to me and trusting me while helping the business grow.

Priyanka and team Notion Press, for bringing the dream come true.

Thank you, family and friends, for making me the person that I am today.

A big thank you to my readers for your love on my debut book. Happy Reading!

ABOUT THE AUTHOR

Garvit Chaharia, a passionate entrepreneur and a financial advisor by profession, resides in the holy city of Varanasi. He is a social animal and a hardcore networker. His love for his work is what made him write this book. Garvit has been in this industry for the past 15 years and his know-how and experience are what this book has to offer.

Health is the biggest wealth and he is a firm believer of the same. Garvit is a fitness freak with a history of transforming from fat to fit with his perseverance and grit. He holds a positive attitude towards everything in life, which paves the way for him to achieve all that he desires through his hardwork, dedication and strong will power. When not updating his knowledge and skill game, Garvit is often found travelling. He awaits your feedback at **garvit@deevaventures.com**

FOREWORD

We all love MONEY. Working towards growing money through the financial service industry that we are in is by far the best in the world for more reasons than one. Keeping the helicopter view in mind, anyone and everyone can take up financial advising as a profession as it doesn't demand much. All one needs is to qualify for an exam which requires basic financial knowledge and pay a small registration amount and turn into a financial advisor overnight. No other capital or infrastructure is required as such. In fact, one can start this business from the comfort of one's own home. This is one of the main reasons why I am fond of this industry too.

Yet, when one takes a closer look, he/she will find out that not many survive in this business. The difficult part is to sustain in this sector and earn a name for oneself. It is very important for a financial advisor to prove his/her own worth to prospective clients before actually engaging them as clients.

According to a survey, 90% of the financial advisors are not successful and end up with nothing, while 7% struggle to sustain. Only 3% of the people thrive and excel in this industry. And this mere 3% is surely doing things which the rest 97% aren't doing. There certainly has to be something different in their workings as compared to others. Also, they are putting in a lot more effort physically and mentally to reach where they are.

The products that we deal in are the same for all financial advisors, be it mutual funds or bonds, insurance or various other investments. But what actually differs is the way each seller sells the product. One cannot keep assuring clients about one's own credentials. You need to create uniqueness in the way you talk about your products and your way of handling clients. Your USP will speak for you and help you outstay your competitors.

I will explain this using a small example. Suppose you are hungry and you are craving for food which can be eaten at various places. It could be in a food court, a roadside stall, a fine dining restaurant or at your own home as well. But you still choose a desired place for it and settle for nothing less. Why is it so? Certainly, for the EXPERIENCE. The experience which no other place can offer you except the one which has always catered to your needs and expectations. The place might not have the best chefs and might as well have food with average taste. But it's still on your priority list. And the reason is the hospitality, the ambience, the presentation which no other place can provide you with. People can pay exorbitantly to get an experience like no other and not for the product alone.

The same applies to any business. Since we cannot do anything different with the product segment, why not try something exceptional with the experience that the client receives while offering you business? Provide your client with a 5-star magical experience like never before. This should be way beyond what your competitors are providing. And once you are able to do this, your clients will carry forward this hassle-free experience verbally to their family and friends.

You cannot be doing the regular, ordinary stuff and expect huge returns. If you keep doing what you have always done, you will keep getting what you have always got. Extra growth only comes in when some extra effort is added in the way you do things differently at your end.

Through this book, I aim to focus on the workings of becoming a successful financial advisor through my experiences. This book will ensure that your business turns into a Pull Business Model from a Push Business Model if you make sure to implement everything discussed here. Your business will become the magnet attracting clients and bringing in deals.

Having been in this industry for over 15 years now, I am more than glad to share my learnings, my research done over the years and experiences with my counterparts, and help them establish themselves and grow in any way possible.

Just reading this book is definitely not going to fetch you success. But a thorough understanding of the book and implementing the secrets shared here over a certain period of time will help you grow your venture manifold.

Growing as a financial advisor is a gradual process. We advise people on one of the most important aspects of their existence, MONEY. Any kind of hurry will only lead to its downfall. Here, we are to advise people on their money matters. One decision gone haywire might end up shaking the financial status of our client. Hence, it is very important to take baby steps in understanding this sector and this book will guide you through the same.

It is a clear insight on how this business should be done. It won't teach you the workings; rather, it will teach you how to work. This book is not here to give you any kind of product knowledge, right pricing technique or guide you through ethical practices. You should already be well-versed with all of these before accessing this book. Only then will you be able to benefit from this book. Simply reading it without any core and theoretical knowledge of the financial world will not be of any use.

This book will give you a totally different perspective of the same business you have been working in for years. This book will help you open your mind and rethink the tactics you have been following to run this business. By the time you finish reading this book, you will have a rich and diverse knowledge about how to establish yourself successfully in the financial sector, and this, in turn, will help you broaden your thought process about the same. And the secrets let out by this book will be found nowhere else. No management schools or product training programs will guide you like this book does.

This book is a summary of my experiences acquired and practiced over the years through trial and error. It is a sum-up of the past 15 years of my professional life. Hence, it will give you more practical knowledge than bookish knowledge. This book will help you speed up on your road to success.

1. STEPPING STONES

"The first step towards getting somewhere is to decide that you are not going to stay where you are."

1.1 GOOD VIBES ONLY

"Vibe high and the magic around you will unfold."

– Akilnathan Logeswaran

Does your being around people make them glad? Is your company a good influence on people? Are people happy when they meet you? The answer to all this should be a big 'YES.' The power of positivity and good vibes has an amazing impact on one's personal and professional lives. It ensures that every moment is worth the experience and every goal worth shooting for. What you contribute to your personal and professional environment is quite important. But how you contribute is the bigger question. You may have vast knowledge of your business and might as well be quite skilful at the same. However, if your approach towards a new client, company representative, an employee or people in social gatherings is negative or rather arrogant, you should be well-prepared to receive the same negativity in the form of declining business opportunities and number of clients.

Vibes are powerful enough to lead you to success or bring you down to failure. The interesting part is the fact that you have the power to choose how you exert your own energy. As humans, we are quick to judge people around us.

Whenever we meet a person, especially for the first time, subconsciously we start rating them in numbers. I call this the 'Plus One – Minus One' formula. Depending on an individual's traits whether positive or negative, we keep scoring them accordingly at the back of our minds. And this is a common practice that we follow with whoever we meet or hear about. Whether we meet them in person or hear about them or follow them on social media, we tend to mark them in positive or negative numbers depending on their behaviour, habits and language. Although it should be the other way round.

Now it's time to evaluate your own self. You need to know what impact you have on people around you. I believe even others rate you for your actions and reactions. The aura that you create in your surroundings in your day-to-day life is what encircles your professional area too. Sometimes, it so happens that you haven't met an individual or done business with them ever, yet they form an opinion about you. They have already given you positive or negative numbers depending on what they have heard about you. This happens because of the feedback they have received about you from the market. And you should be well aware that this feedback actually originates from you, from your place of work and from your immediate people. So it's totally upon you to control this review. Be aware of how you carry yourself and your way of conversing with people of all stature. This will generate positives and negatives for you. You might do a hundred good deeds before people praise you, but one bad action from your end and the same people will turn a lot of positive points into negative numbers.

This holds true for your team members as well. How they go about carrying your business with other people is also of much importance. They are actually your representatives and work on your behalf. So all the plus ones and minus ones that they collect in the industry are actually collectively yours.

An actual situation will help you understand this better. Suppose you have never been on time for anything in your entire life. Right from school parent-teacher meetings (PTMs) to college parties and carrying it forward to business events, you have forever been unpunctual. This, to a large extent, makes your friends and acquaintances believe and accept that you will always be late, irrespective of the importance of the event. And in no time, the word will spread about you being an unpunctual and irresponsible person. Furthermore, it will lead to people co-relating your habits to your business and deducing that you are an irresponsible professional who never fulfils work commitments on time. Factually, it might not be true, yet it would be enough to pull you and your business down.

Likewise, if you are always organised, personally and professionally, it will leave a positive impact on others. Right from getting up on time to keeping your things in place, if you are disciplined about your lifestyle and work, word will spread around. People will start associating you with organised business sense too. This will garner positive points for you and push you up in the numbers game.

Making sure that the vibes flow in your favour is a well-thought and planned move. And this plan needs to be activated and carried out on multiple platforms like social media, work place, your team and also socially. Word of mouth does wonders for every business and it would do the same for your business if you are able to create your own positive space in the minds of people around you. It starts right from your home, office and close-knit family and friends. The way you carry and handle yourself in various situations is the key to creating a healthy environment. Your family, friends, clients and your competitors too should have a feel-good factor about you surrounding them. The conversations that you make, the mails and messages that you send, or any other form of communication that happens from your end should yield positivity and good vibes. It should make the receiver feel good about himself and you too.

Once you are able to achieve this, there is no looking back. This is the time when business will start flowing in and you will be the one reaping the profits.

"Vibes are powerful enough to lead to your success or bring you down to your failures."

1.2 CHOOSE YOUR GROUND

"When you speak to everyone, you speak to no one."

– Meredith Hill

As beginners, you all will be happy with any customer that walks in through your door. Though it's only with time that you will realise that not all clients are assets for your business. Some even prove to be a liability. Hence, as a business owner, you should be selective in customer selection.

The primary step in any business is to define your market and client base. And if I talk about our business, i.e. financial advising, this is one of the most crucial steps. Customer strategy is the key to success in the financial market as your clients give you business according to your credibility. Wrong choice of clients will ultimately lead to the downfall of your business and, to avoid this, you must choose your clients with utmost caution.

To know whom to choose as your client, you must first know yourself. See what size of business you are capable of handling. Are you competent enough to face your counterparts? Are you adept enough to manage the funds of the clients you are aiming at? Do you have the confidence and calibre to handle and minimise the risks involved in your client's business? Will your personality be effective on your target customers? Is your proficiency in the financial sector worth the funds that you are planning to invest on your customer's behalf? Do your resources and infrastructure allow you to handle big portfolios? And if you are doubtful about any of the above, it's time that you reconsider your client base.

If you are eyeing the elite crowd, the high net-worth individuals (HNI), and are keen on handling their big portfolios and managing their huge bank balances, you need to evaluate yourself first. You need to judge whether you are worthy of being given the responsibility that you are expecting. Reason out if you would trust a person like yourself to handle your own finances. If not, then first become a person of that stature. Invest in upgrading your financial knowledge as well as management skills. Become the professional whose personality assures the clients of his capabilities. Why would anybody hand over an eight-figure cheque to somebody inept?

There are many people in this industry who think that working from home could also bring them business. But this is not true for financial advisors who want to grow and do a sizeable amount of business. In today's times, showbiz is as important as capabilities. It's quite important for you to invest in your infrastructure, manpower and also technology. You need to upgrade your office as much as you upgrade yourself. Your clients should be able to understand the kind of business that you do by having a look at your workplace. From being well-furnished and organised to being technologically advanced, your workplace speaks volumes about you. These investments will only lead to bigger clients and higher revenues.

Another important aspect that I would like to mention is marketing. How you promote your brand is really important. Until you advertise yourself, your prospective clients will not be well-versed with your calibre and all your efforts will be of no use. So, it's necessary for you to let people know what you are capable of.

But if you do not have the resources, infrastructure and manpower to handle big clients, start by handling small portfolios. Because, if you aim higher than what you are capable of, you will end up only wasting time, energy and resources. This will take you nowhere. If you're incapable and go to a big client, then you might earn yourself a negative score. Your limitedness won't let him give you business and it might forever close doors for you. Instead, gradually upgrade yourself professionally and personally, and then aim for bigger clients when they cannot refuse you.

The same applies otherwise. If you are well-equipped with all the resources, then you shouldn't settle for less. This will restrict you from higher revenues which you actually deserve. So, you should choose your client base keeping in mind your own stature.

Another parameter is to divide the selected client base into different groups depending on their profession, geographical location or income slabs. There are various reasons behind this. For instance, if you take up an industrial area as your prospective client base, you could get a good number of clients there itself, and there will be no need for you to explore other geographical locations immediately. Adding to your ease would be the type of products that they would demand. Most of them would have similar requirements, which would save you time and energy.

If we divide prospective clients according to their profession, it's easier to convert clients of one profession be it doctors, lawyers, chartered accountants, salaried individuals, businessmen, etc. If your customer base is jewellers, supposedly, then they all would require insurance for their store and they would hedge gold. This would lead us to becoming experts in this area by working with so many clients, which in turn would create goodwill for us. Hence, even more customers from the same trade.

If we choose people of a particular community or society, then even that will smoothen the conversion process. If you belong to that particular community or society or know people who belong there, it will help you to develop a relationship with them. This further has a possibility of converting your acquaintances into your clients. And then, people known to your acquaintances will also come into contact with you. In my case, most of my clients are businessmen as I belong to a business family. Hence, you should always first try for clients near you or known to you and then expand your boundaries.

Once you have figured out your client base, evaluate your decision. See if you have enough people who fit your client base. Selecting the clientele will give you clarity on whom to focus on and how to sell successfully. Getting new clients is an ongoing process. But knowing where to look for your target clients will make the process easier.

"Judge whether you are worthy of being given the responsibility that you are expecting."

1.3 NETWORK = NET WORTH

"Networking is not collecting contacts.
Networking is about planting relations."

– Unknown

Networking is the core of every business. It helps you form strong business relationships and earn a good reputation, and helps to create endless business opportunities. It is vital for growth. If you are new to a business, it can help you establish it or help grow an existing one.

Clearly, if you aren't taking out time to meet and communicate with people who aren't your clients, you are missing out on some huge opportunities which would have otherwise proved to be beneficial for your business.

So, how and where exactly do you start networking? Now that you know who your target customer is, you need to try every ethical way that could turn him into your client. To understand this concept better, you need to revisit your college days wherein you did every possible thing to attract your person of interest. If you can recall, you must have chosen the coaching class wherein you found more people of the opposite gender. You tried to put in extra effort too if you had zeroed upon your choice. Even if it meant enrolling yourself in a dance class where he/she was a student, irrespective of your interest in that class.

Likewise, you need to find places where your prospective clients visit on a regular basis. You need to find out which clubs they are a member of and which social and networking organisations they belong to, so that you can set up a chance meeting with your to-be client. It could be a social club or a gym or even a temple where the client visits on a regular basis. You need to first procure the membership of these clubs and social organisations where you are sure to find and meet your prospective clients. You can join clubs like Rotary International, JCI, Round Table, BNI, etc. These clubs pave a path for strong business networking. Opting for leadership roles in these clubs is also a way to earn the limelight. The idea here is not only to be seen but to also be visible in the positive light. Work hard to earn yourself a position and maintain it. This will lead people to trust you more and bank upon your advice.

For instance, when I wanted to expand my geographical boundaries and move from Varanasi to an adjacent area like Bhadohi, I first found links to join the All India Carpet Manufacturers Association (AICMA). It is an organisation that has carpet manufacturers and exporters, as well as people directly and indirectly linked with the carpet business, as its members. I became a member of this organisation to handle the manufacturers' marine insurance and product liability insurance. I hosted an introductory seminar and sent out invites for the same. That is how I formed a network amongst its members and gradually started handling their personal portfolios as well. This is how networking helps you get new clients and grow your business manifold.

Once you have become a member of the important clubs and organisations, it's now time to start collecting data of the people whom you are considering to approach. You need to work on the data extensively. The numbers collected should be in line with the available resources. Even if you have managed to collect more data than your appetite, it's advisable to select a few of them and work on them. The rest can be stored for future use. You should be well-informed about their contact number, date of birth, official address and email IDs. All this data can be gathered from social media, club or organisation directories, company websites and also from friends and family. This data will help you ease out the process of contacting them and sending out mails and messages. This will also set the base to establish a strong relationship with your clients in the near future. And how this can happen will be discussed in the following chapters.

You can also opt to go to trade fairs, expos and exhibitions organised in your city. There you will get to meet people in huge numbers and you can segregate your client base according to your appetite and collect all the necessary data then and there itself.

From group meetings to one-on-one sessions, these chance meetings are really helpful in setting up new business relations. Individual meet-ups also prove to be beneficial depending on client approach.

Like this one time when I converted a very important client while sweating it out in the gym with him. Such a fortuitous encounter with your client could lead to big business opportunities if utilised in the best way.

Your mailer lists and broadcast messages will also have a huge database as a result of networking. Now, it's up to you to make good use of your meet-and-greet moments. These networking circles will in turn increase your net worth by increasing your clients and business year after year. The more you network, the higher your net worth.

"The idea here is not only to be seen but to also be visible in the positive light."

1.4 DATE YOUR CLIENT

"The key is when a customer walks away, thinking, 'Wow, I love doing business with them, and I want to tell others about the experience.'"

– Shep Hyken

To be a financial advisor, you need to be a people's person. And this is what makes me love this profession as I get to meet and interact with strangers on a regular basis. These strangers bond over coffee and conversations to form new business relationships. These connections are unique in their own way. You must be amazed to know that I look at them as a bond between couples. Having said this, I would like to further elaborate on how a relationship between a financial advisor and a client is similar to that between two individuals who are fond of each other.

A lot of effort is required to form a new bond and keep it strong, and the same is the case here. You must constantly endeavour if you are to make a new client and succeed in it. Just like you need to impress your love interest in a lot of ways, similarly, you need to work on ways to influence your client. You need to build the required trust that lays the foundation of any relationship and also retain this trust over the years. Being loyal and faithful towards them will do the bit. Give time to each client individually and focus on their needs and requirements.

Here, the collected information about your clients will come handy too. First and foremost, you need to save their contact numbers on your phone along with important details. Before finding your spot on their phone, reserve one for them in your device. This way, the client will not need to introduce himself when he calls. This practice makes them feel important. Saving their birthdays and other important dates along with their contact will remind you of the particular day itself and you can wish them without fail. This call to wish them is not only to make them happy. Look at it as a very big opportunity for you to grab as it's a special day for them.

Being informed about your prospective client's vehicle number by now could also turn out to be useful. Here's the catch. If you know the vehicle number and find their vehicle in some gatherings or clubs, that's your chance to plan out the conversation that you have to make with them when you meet them face to face in the gathering. This will help you prepare yourself in advance. You could also get lucky by looking out for the client whom you haven't been able to meet otherwise. After locating their car, you can make a little effort and find them in the gathering.

Knowing a client's travel plans is an added advantage. This will help coincide with yours accordingly, in case you have the same destination plans too. This is something I tried during my college days. I made my travel arrangements after finding out about my love interest's plans. I was able to grab her attention and make good conversation with her during the flight. Eventually, we became good friends on board. Imagine getting a couple of hours with your client when he has nothing else to do on board. It could turn out to be a really profitable business meeting and help you convert deals. All this can happen only when you have all the data collected beforehand.

Their fitness routine, their office timings, etc. can also be helpful. This will let you meet your clients at home or at the office accordingly, and during morning or evening walks.

So, if you still believe in the old school way of going to a client's office and asking to set up a meeting, sorry to disappoint you folks. This traditional outlook doesn't work anymore. These new ways of setting up chance meetings with your clients and never leaving an opportunity to impress them works better. It may take some time but these methods will definitely reap clients for you.

In a relationship, you don't lose your patience. When you really like the other person, you are ready to wait for months before you actually become friends with them. Likewise, I advise you to be patient and, most importantly, keep trying. Don't expect people to turn into your clients overnight. The process may take time. Some clients may take days, a few might take months, while a handful will take even years to convert. But, self-restraint is the key. And the wait will be worth it.

I have tasted success with a couple of clients after three to five years of working on them. And a client, I recall, was eyed upon by me for the past seven years and I was finally able to convert him after all the wait. There are a few clients who are there in my prospective list but yet to be converted even after a decade of trying. My optimistic approach towards my venture makes me still work on them and am sure of cracking them some day.

The point is to work on each client individually. The strategy might differ from one client to another but the basic point is to collect information and use them to your best capability. Treat each client as one important relationship and you will see how things change for the better.

"Just like you need to impress your love interest in a lot of ways, similarly you need to work on ways to influence your client."

1.5 DON'T INTRODUCE YOURSELF

"You don't get a second chance to make a first impression."

– James Uleman

Your first impression in front of your client is very important as it forms your image in the mind of your client. It is generally formed as the result of a conversation between the both of you, though it can also be created from just catching a glimpse of you. Within the first seven seconds of meeting, your clients will form a solid impression about you and make 11 important decisions. However, some research suggests a tenth of a second is all it takes to start determining traits like trustworthiness. And by this you must have got an idea that this isn't enough time to talk about who you are and what you do, impress your new client or make any initial blunders.

Your first meeting or phone call is the deciding factor of your fate with the client. So it should be planned way in advance. There should be no room for mistakes. The first conversation that you have with your client should leave a lasting and positive impact on him. It's repulsive to receive a phone call during business hours and listen to the other person introducing and marketing himself. This is a totally wrong approach.

The right way is to first make the customer aware about you and your business. Before you decide to make that first call or fix that first meeting, you should be confident that your client has received all the necessary information about you. This includes your name, your nature of business, your social standing, your volume of business and the clients you have. Otherwise, you are sure to waste half of your scheduled call or meeting in introducing yourself and your business. This precious time could be utilised in impressing your client instead.

You must now be wondering how you would do this exactly. This is where social media plays a very important role. Your Facebook and other social media handles, your WhatsApp broadcasts and bulk messages and emails should be self-introductory and self-explanatory. Doing only this is not enough though.

Another important factor is to find out common links with your prospective clients and use them for reference. It's very beneficial that you find common connections between you and your client. It could be your friends or extended family; in some cases, even acquaintances work. A referral from your existing client does wonders too. This way you can ask them to refer you to your new clients. Targeting your clients in terms of referrals is very tricky. Hence, it should be planned with caution.

Whenever you eye a new customer, it's best to first put him on all your broadcast lists and add him on all your social media handles. Make yourself visible enough for him to notice you. Give enough time to yourself and to him. Be sure that he knows about you and your business before you decide to make that first call. If in doubt, use your network and find referrals. But do not move forward before this most important step.

Doing the reverse of first setting up a meeting and introducing yourself will only waste your time and his. In fact, it might lead to a negative impression about you being created in your client's mind.

You would rather want your client to exchange pleasantries with you instead of asking you who you are and what you do. Your client will also have a clear insight about your stature and will not misunderstand in any way. He will also be prepared to a certain extent for his first business meeting with you.

It is so much better to first put all your efforts in doing the homework and find your goal half-achieved than using all your energy in the ground.

"The first conversation that you have with your client should leave a lasting and positive impact on him."

1.6 HOME IN PHONE

"In today's modern world, people are either asleep or on their cell phones."

– Unknown

Mobile phones are the new age necessity of life. It's very hard to find a person without a mobile phone these days. From calls and messages to entertainment and news, everything has come down to our mobile phone. A person of any age or stature feels handicapped without the digital phone. This small gadget has taken the financial world by storm too. Most of the successful financial advisors even have their own applications. To get a space, a home in the client's cell phone is half the job done. It is of utmost importance to get your client to save your contact number on his phone. The mails and the messages that you send to your client's number might be ignored or spammed if your contact is not saved on their phone. To get them delivered to their inbox, you have to make sure that your number is saved correctly on their phone first.

The first step towards this is to create your contact card and keep it ready in your phonebook. How you build this contact card is really important. It should be

Mohit Kumar | Deeva Ventures Pvt Ltd
Relationship Manager

Mutual Funds, Life Insurance, Health Insurance,
General Insurance, Bonds, Fixed Deposits,
Stock Broking, Loans Etc.

Personal Phone
+91 98000 00000

Office Phone
+91 98000 00000

Personal Email
mohit@deevaventures.com

Office Email
info@deevaventures.com

Website
https://www.deevaventures.com

Address
D - 123, XYZ Tower
ABC Road
Varanasi - 221001

well-planned and saved with your complete details. Or else, your client might not find your number in spite of having your contact on his phone. Your name, company's name, contact number, alternate number (if any), your office number, official email ID, website address and official postal address. Be sure to mention the nature of your business. It might so happen that your prospective client doesn't remember your name but tries to connect you with your profession. The nature of your business (in our case, insurance or investments) mentioned in your contact card will help him find your number on his phone.

The next step is to get that contact card saved into your prospective client's device. All the devices are flooded with spam messages and calls nowadays. Most of the people have stopped receiving calls from unknown numbers for the sole reason of being disturbed by telemarketers. Even if the call is from a celebrity or a known person, you might ignore the call if the number is not saved on your device. Hence, if your contact card is saved on the client's phone before you call, this will help the person know who the caller is. And he will pick up your call most likely. Even if the other person misses your call due to certain reasons, he might call you back knowing that the caller was you. But all this can happen only when your number is saved on his phone. This can be tricky but extremely beneficial.

If your number is not on his phone, he will not be informed of your calls at all. Irrespective of his desire to work with you or not, he should be aware of your calls to him. So, if and when he wishes to take financial services, you should be his first choice. Moreover, if you happen to meet him, this can be a conversation starter for you.

A common mistake which people make while sharing their contact is to give a missed call to the other person. Some give their visiting cards, while few others dictate their numbers and ask the other person to save it. All this will prove to be futile if your client forgets to save the number or saves it with a couple of wrong digits or name. Hence, the better practice is to send your prospective client the contact card which will get saved instantly without any error. Contact cards can especially be shared while you are networking or socialising with your prospective clients.

Once the contact card is saved on your customer's phone, the probability of your call being answered increases by 50%. The next big challenge is to not make this one a telemarketing call. If you make a similar call, be ready to create negativity in your buyer's mind. If you have to introduce yourself for the first five minutes, the customer might not be interested at all and would hang up the phone with a lot of negativity for you and your company.

So, there is a little preparation that is to be done before making that first phone call to your client. Send a message and/or email to your client, along with your contact card citing all the relevant details. This should include a brief introduction about you and your company, the nature of

Varanasi's No 1 Financial Market Place | Deeva Ventures Pvt Ltd | Introduction
We help investors manage their Wealth, by
youtube.com

Dear **Sir,**

We expertise in helping investors manage their **Wealth**, by providing disciplined advisory on **Portfolio Management, Risk Management & Debt Management.**

Click here to know more about us.
https://youtu.be/uB-Ub8obf0Q

*I am **Mohit** and I will help you with SIP Investment..*

Kindly save my contact card in your phone so that you don't miss my call & email.

Regards,
Mohit Kumar
Relationship Manager
Deeva Ventures Pvt Ltd

www.deevaventures.com

INVESTMENT | LOAN | INSURANCE

Mohit Kumar | Deeva Ventures Pvt Ltd

Message Add contact

your business, a link to your website and how you can help them. Make sure your team also follows the same procedure before placing a call to the client. Don't expect a reply in return as most of the clients don't respond.

But at least the message and mail from your end will leave them with an expectation that you will call. I have been practicing this since the past few years now and my calls are being received more than ever. As compared to the calls which I made earlier, the call receiving rate presently has gone up by 75%.

After doing the above mentioned, you are good to make that first call to your client. We will now talk about how to handle your first call. When the client receives the call, you are required to ask him for an appointment after exchanging pleasantries. And if you are lucky enough, the client will give you an appointment for a meeting with him. After thanking him for the same, you need to send an email and a message to your client mentioning the said date and time of the meeting. One of the applications that are there to schedule meetings can also be used while fixing an appointment with your client. This will save the date and time automatically in the client's calendar too.

This email/message will act as a reminder for him and the probability of the meeting being held will increase. In case of any change of date or time for the meeting from the client's end, the client will likely reschedule it and inform you of the same.

Your Meeting for 'Term Insurance' is scheduled

Mohit | Deeva Ventures Pvt Ltd
rohit@xyz.com

Meeting.ics
ICS-456 B

Dear **Rohit Kumar,**

Greetings!!!

As discussed, our meeting for **Term Insurance** is scheduled on **21/06/2021 16:15.**

Our representative, **Mohit Kumar** will get in touch with you.

Kindly make yourself available for the Meeting.

Thanks & Regards,

Deeva Ventures Pvt Ltd.
D - 123, XYZ Tower
ABC Road, Varanasi - 221001
Ph: +919800000000
Email: info@deevaventures.com
Website: www.deevaventures.com

INVESTMENT | LOAN | INSURANCE

Click below to save in the calendar

In case he asks you to call a month later or so, do set up a reminder for the same. This will not let you miss out on the client and, in turn, on the business that he might give you. This is because the client is always on the lookout for different ways to say no to you and you need to try all possible ways to convert this into yes. For this, a follow-up is a must. This will turn tables for you and clients might agree to meet you eventually.

At times, it might so happen that a client stops picking your calls. That is the time for you to stop. There is a very thin line between following up with your clients and irritating them with your calls. You need to identify this and act accordingly. The second call should always be made after a gap of 15 days since the first call, the third after a month of the second call. And this gap should go on increasing if your calls are being ignored by the client. Take a break and make a fresh start all over again.

Be a smart businessman and ensure to attract your clients by your moves and calls, and not make them repelled by you and your business strategies.

"Even if the call is from a celebrity or a known person, you might ignore the call if the number is not saved on your device."

1.7 ABOUT THE FIRST MEETING

"Hope More, Expect Less."

– Unknown

The first client meeting is not actually a business meeting. It is more of an introductory meeting and should remain so. This meeting should be utilised to sell your own self so that you are successful in selling your products in the subsequent meetings.

You should be impeccably dressed from head to toe. This will be your first physical image in your client's mind and will remain so forever. The importance of reaching on time is still underestimated in India but it should actually be otherwise. People who are punctual have a different fan following altogether. This is sure to earn you respect.

You get brownie points for being a good listener in the first meeting. Because, this meeting demands so. A lot of financial advisors make this mistake of talking too much. They think that explaining all their products at one go will earn them business. But this is a misconception. The right approach is to first hear your client out. I believe that 80% of the conversation should be from your client's end and 20% should be from your end. Ask small questions and wait for the client to divulge the basics. Don't trust yourself to remember everything. Rather, note down pointers of all that the client lets out as it will help you prepare for your future meetings. Know his needs and requirements. Explain your products well and observe his area of interest. Analyse the depth of your client's portfolio and try to understand his investment plans. Try to learn if he is already investing with a competitor of yours. If your findings suggest this, try to dig into the details of who the competitor is (in a subtle way). Go slow. Being fast will only lead you to lost opportunities. You should understand the importance of effective communication and act accordingly.

Clarity in communication is the key to any successful relationship. Be it personal or professional, every relationship has certain expectations which are built through communication and demands for them to be fulfilled.

Expectation setting towards a client is critical for any business. Whether you sell cars, run a restaurant or invest for people, your customers want to have set expectations so that they can plan accordingly. The size of commitment is not primary. The fulfilment of the commitment made is what holds utmost importance. Setting realistic customer expectations helps a business win the customer's trust. And the foundation for this should be laid in the first meeting itself.

This can be very well explained through a real life situation. On a beautiful Sunday morning, you inform your family about spending the whole day together and ending it with a nice dinner. Your wife and kids are overjoyed and start giving their suggestions and all of you set out to execute the plans. After half a day, you receive an urgent business call and you end up bringing everybody home abruptly without even feeding them dinner. How do you think your family takes it? They will definitely be annoyed and might not want to trust you a second time when you promise something. But if you keep the promise and also treat them with ice-cream while returning home, their happiness will soar high because you gave them more than expected.

The same is true in business. When a client ends up being dissatisfied, it is because he was fed with wrong expectations and was waiting for them to be fulfilled. This will eventually lead to conflict and lost business.

It is, in fact, advised to set low expectations. So much of our life's disappointment comes from the unrealistic expectations that we set for ourselves. Even a minute 500-rupee haircut can bring disappointment to a person if it doesn't end up the way he had imagined or wanted it to be. When it comes to setting expectations, always under-commit and over-deliver. Because, if you are able to successfully manage this, you can meet your expectations and exceed them too. As a result, you will have a long-term relationship with your client and, if you are lucky enough, he might advocate for you too. Setting just the right assumptions and delivering what you commit is the key to any successful business.

A lot of people are not good at communicating with their clients. Few advisors also feel that making big promises will sell their products faster. They have a habit of boasting about their infrastructure, team, technology and big clientele. When actually, none of these are true. They also believe in setting unrealistic goals for their clients so that they can have a huge client base. But what they don't realise is that this success is short-lived. The client might get impressed in the first go and give you business. But when he doesn't receive the returns promised, he will not trust you again and strip you of your business. There will be no second chance for you. This will lead to the downfall of your business.

It is totally unfair to promise a huge percentage of returns. Some advisors suggest 15-30% returns on equity. If you belong to this category, you need to change your direction right away. Making false commitments like this will take you nowhere. You cannot control the market and expect your clients to get huge returns. It is all momentary. In fact, it would be sensible for you to promise 8-12% returns over a period of 5-7 years (owing to market conditions). This might prove to be a little difficult in winning over new clients but it is definitely a smart move to retain your clients.

When talking about Systematic Investment Plans (SIPs), remember to set the client's expectations so that they run their SIPs for a longer period of time. I always suggest my clients to run their SIPs for a lifetime.

In case of insurance, don't commit returns that are not guaranteed by the company. Don't set high expectations in case of claims as regards to time and amount. Commit only those things that are in your control. Expectations cannot be assured, and make sure to communicate this well to your clients.

Immediate opening of accounts under all circumstances, policy creation process, redemption process and easing out the documentation process are few of the false commitments which many of the investors make. But false expectations are short-lived. Also, promising them cashless, easy and timely claim settlement procedures will only pile up on the false expectations that you set up.

An honest and sensible approach may take some time to fetch you clients. Nevertheless, this is here to stay. You will get healthy and long-lasting business relationships as returns for setting up the right expectations for your clients. Commit all that is in your control and not beyond that. Promising things over and above your capacity is a blunder that none should commit.

This first meeting should be utilised in establishing your credibility in front of your client. Don't expect or do business in the first meeting itself. Leave it for the second meeting. The first one is to understand the client and his requirements. It is also to lay down the right expectations so that it sets up the base for consecutive meetings. It should wind up only after trying to set the time and date for the second meeting.

"The size of commitment is not primary. The fulfilment of the commitment made is what holds utmost importance."

2. THE PATH TO FOLLOW

"Make it simple, but significant."

– Don Draper

2.1 RAIN OR SHINE

"Rain, hail or shine, success is mine."

– Unknown

Does your employee not take a salary when you don't have profitable business? Does your rent stop when your business takes a back seat? Do your personal expenses take a break when your competitor grabs your business? Do other factors like product fails or market crashes put a halt to any of your overheads?

If the answer to all the above questions is a "NO," then your business model should be the one which reaps profits for you all year round. I call it the 'RAIN & SHINE' model. Your business should be such that it earns revenues for you in all seasons so that you can pay your bills, salaries, rent and EMIs on time. Your business model should also be able to save for you and your family so as to lead a life of your dreams. Your business model is the engine which will drive your business to heights. Hence, plan it well before you execute it to reap profits.

Let me tell you a story to understand this in a better way. Once, there was a village with no water of its own. The villagers had to go to a lake which was 5 km away and fetch buckets of water from there, every day. Two men, Rohit and Mohit, who had returned from the city, tried to find a solution to this and ease out the process for the villagers. Rohit immediately got to work and started getting buckets of water to the village every morning and selling it for Rs 5/bucket. His business was an instant hit.

On the other hand, Mohit vanished from the village only to return after a month with two other men. He had hired labourers to dig a pipeline from the lake to the village. He put a tap at the village's end of the pipeline and the villagers could fill their buckets at Rs 2/bucket. Now, the villagers turned to him for water as he charged 60% lesser than Rohit and was available 24*7.

This tells us that Rohit's success was only temporary. Mohit took a little time to get started but then it was forever. While Rohit was more hard-working, Mohit had proper planning before he started. And this is what gave Mohit more business than Rohit. So, it is for you to decide whether you want to be more hard-working or smarter.

Proper planning is very crucial to a successful business model. Right forethought can only lead to an organised business set-up. This will lead you to move forward and earn revenues throughout the year. This book will teach you the four fundamentals behind every business model and its execution. It is very important to select the right client as discussed previously. Choice of products is the next important thing. And also having the right strategy behind offering the right product to the right client is where the trick lies. This is not enough though. The timing should also be right as to when you should offer a particular product to a particular client. If you miss out on planning on any of the four elements or if you fail to execute the plan rightly, your business may not grow as much as it should.

In this book, I will let out secrets behind the proper planning of your financial business. Only with proper organisation will your business generate revenues and help you grow year after year, in spite of any challenges that might come your way. As you progress with this book, it will teach you various ways to make your business model an all-season profit-rearing model.

"Your business should be such that it earns revenues for you in all seasons so that you can pay your bills, salaries, rent and EMIs on time."

2.2 TURN THE TABLES AROUND

"Success as a therapist is not found in doing something for the client, but rather in being someone for the client."

– Ili Rivera Walter

Businesses all over the world require different workings to survive and become successful. Few rely on hard work and determination while others take a lot more than that. Manufacturing and trading majorly demand infrastructure and funds. Once these factors are sorted, one can open a unit or store and start selling. Advertisement and goodwill add up to these factors and help the business become a profitable and successful venture. But this doesn't hold true for all kinds of businesses.

In a venture like ours, the relationship with the client plays a major role. For this reason and more, financial consultancy is considered to be one of the most competitive and difficult out of all professions in the world. Resources are crucial and goodwill too, but these alone cannot run a financial advising firm. Having strong business relationships is the key to becoming a successful consultant. A lot of hard work and effort is required for the same. It definitely takes time to establish bonds, but it surely pays off in the long run and is worth the wait.

As advised earlier, you need to join various social and networking organisations to develop bonds and further take it to the next level. Your communication skills, social behaviour, the aura that you create around you, all of these contribute to the connections that you establish over a period of time. You need to understand how much your relationship with your prospective client needs to grow to reach a level of trust. You need to figure out the turning point of your bond which will lead your business to grow manifold. You need to plan well in advance the roadmap which will lead to each of your clients. How much effort and work is required in the case of each client is to be chalked out so as to get fruitful business out of them.

Though, your business will not survive on relationships alone. The trust that you build upon your customers and your market credibility that you establish over time is what truly pulls the clients towards you. Both of these are very important to retain your clients and have a long-lasting business relationship with them. And it is a well-known fact that getting into a relationship is very easy. Doesn't take too much to get introduced and make a new friend. But what's tricky is keeping the spark alive. Maintaining the bond well is what tests your true colours.

In business too, you need to be one step ahead of your client every day. You need to become your client's friend and eventually like his family member. When you get closely connected with your client, you will get access to his financial portfolio and needs ahead of time. You will be aware of his requirements even before he asks you for it. You will eventually become one amongst his go-to people for any financial advice. You will need to be that one person whom he trusts blindly, especially in matters of funds and investments.

Such should be your influence on him. Sitting on opposite sides of the table like an advisor and a client will only fetch you a mere amount of business. Your growth at this point will be gradual. Instead, work towards becoming as close as his family member who shares the same side of the table as his client. This will earn you multiplied business and your growth will be rapid henceforth.

Your competitors will start to envy you and be overshadowed by your aura. This will create a sense of inferiority in the other consultants around you. They will believe that trying with a client who is close to you is of no use because of the visible bond that you both share. So, in any case, this is a win-win situation for you.

"Become your client's friend and, eventually, like his family member."

2.3 PRODUCT WISE

"Where focus goes energy flows."

– Unknown

The beauty of life lies in its regularity. When it comes to our health, we go for a walk, workout, eat nutritious food and get a good night's sleep every day. Why do we do this? Because, these activities lead to a healthy life and longevity. The same analogy is applicable for businesses too.

Any business requires a regular stream of revenue which will take care of expenses and the remainder will turn into profits. This stuff requires quite an effort; it's no rocket science though. The key here is to become product-wise. Choose the right set of products which will enable you to generate a steady inflow of revenue. I'm sure you deal with a huge arena of products. The product basket usually consists of Mutual Funds, Life Insurance, Health Insurance and General Insurance. In addition, you may also be catering to Stock Broking, Fixed Deposit (FD) & Bonds, National Pension Scheme (NPS), Loans, etc.

For starters, look into your array of products and do a thorough analysis. Life insurance is not warranted to give you regular revenues. These plans usually tend to give high incentives but just for the first premium. They do not stretch beyond that. Also, you cannot expect clients to take up an insurance policy every year because not everybody can bear the burden.

Talking about Mutual Funds, the clientusually does not invest in lump sum amounts every time. I recommend you to prefer SIPs which are not sizeable chunks but recurring in nature. When it comes to Mutual Funds, you always need to focus on an increase in your SIP books resulting in increased Asset Under Management (AUM). SIPs are a great way to reach a grand AUM figure. It is definitely a slow path but also a wise choice because of its stable nature and regularity in income. The incentives in Mutual Funds are not very high because of lower AUM in the initial years of your career. Hence, you need to think of other alternatives too as otherwise it would get difficult for you to cover your expenses.

Avoid depending only on equity funds. If your AUM is equity driven, a crash in the stock market will lead to your revenues taking the brunt. Perhaps, you can try to diversify your client's Mutual Funds portfolio with debt and hybrid funds. This will help the client gain stable returns in the long run, ultimately keeping your income intact. A balanced portfolio also carries an added advantage of being relatively free from stock market fluctuations. Also, don't ignore Liquid Funds as most of the advisors do. It certainly gives comparatively lower revenue but helps in getting clients on board. The volume of business can be increased manifold if attention is paid to Liquid Funds.

Now, let's talk about Stock Broking. This is quite speculative in nature. I have seen a lot of clients incur heavy losses in markets and simply walk out of the door. When this happens, you need to hunt for new clients. No speculator has survived in the market for very long. It is a cash crop so long as the investor is active in the market. Instead, focus on long-term investments so that your client stays intact. Hedging commodities and currencies in this market, on the other hand, is a stable and regular source of revenue.

Your next opportunity is Health Insurance. This product gives incentives every year, but it is limited in a way that clients do not take up new policies every year. One client will not buy more than one health insurance policy. Hence, this is restrictive to the total number of clients that you have onboard. The volume is not very high in this case but the nature of revenue is quite stable and regular.

Next in the line is General Insurance. The investor's business and automobile insurance are much more viable. Even when the client has other expenses to cater to, the above insurance policies continue to be renewed. As a client's business grows his assets grow, thereby resulting in your business growth too. It is a witnessed trend that never in the history of any financial crisis has the General Insurance business taken a hit. The clients always make sure to renew all their insurance policies because they cannot afford additional risks during such tough times. So, this is a product that you should definitely work upon since it has the capability to give you a regular and sizeable amount of business. The insurance business is quite tricky but with the right capability you can reap good benefits.

Apart from all this, there are certain other products such as Bonds and FDs which generate decent revenues. NPS is another segment which is a loss-making product, yet I suggest you to go with it. These are all must haves in the product basket to fulfil your client's requirements.

The product basket can be broadly divided into personal finance and business finance. Personal finance can be irregular and also give lower volume of business. On the other hand, business finance is a regular thing accompanied by a higher volume of business.

A general thumb rule is to have a plethora of products and services. This will help you maximise regular income. The usual mistake that advisors make is that they focus on products which earn higher revenues but they fail to realise that it could be for a short term. Hencc, I suggest you to always focus on the product basket which enables your business to generate regular flow of business for longer periods of time, irrespective of the revenue.

"Any business requires a regular stream of revenue which will take care of expenses and the remainder will turn into profits."

2.4 STAND OUT

"Don't ever go with the flow. Be the flow."

– Unknown

In our industry, people are quick to follow the herd. Yes, you read that right. The herd here being the bunch of advisors who give advice that any other advisor can give. Don't follow the majority: instead, focus on choosing the right way. Stand out from the crowd. You need to differentiate yourself from others. You need to ponder over what makes you right and the other person wrong, or, why should a client choose you over any other Tom, Dick and Harry. You have to be unique with the advice that you give and this can be done only by explaining your thought process to your clients. They have to understand clearly why you are suggesting a certain investment over others and what your reasoning is behind it. Not everybody likes to play the long-term game; think long-term and you will stand out.

There is traffic every day in the financial sector. The markets are flooded with a bunch of new products and companies. The industry is ever evolving. With the introduction of online marketing channels, tech has made it easy for any company to have a voice and reach out to a large pool of prospective investors with the help of social media and various other marketing channels. These companies are using a mix of heterogeneous go-to market strategies and trying to ring a bell in the ears of each individual. The process has become so much easier. The end goal behind the strategy of the company advertising their newest product is to gain customer attention and install curiosity within the customer, and then feed him all the relevant data. The ultimate motive behind all this is to sell their products and earn revenues. And this is done in such a convincing manner that the client starts believing that the new product is what they were always waiting for and prefers it over and above the existing products.

Organisations hire relationship managers to approach channel partners like us to introduce their new offering or a new company. As a financial advisor, the companies approach us to push their products and suggest them to every other investor.

Now, let's look at it from the investors' perspective. The potential investor comes across a new company or old established organisations offering new products every day. The usual touch-points are newspaper/TV advertisements, social media, cold calls, agents, email, marketing, etc. Now when he comes across this new offering or a new company, he is thrilled, he is excited, his eyes are shining seeing that advertisement assuring better returns and irresistible products. The next step, he pulls out his mobile phone to do one of two things: call his financial advisor or Google more about the product/ company.

I often get enquiries from my client seeking more information about the new products in the market; they cannot wait to hear about it. I mostly reply with a NO. As an advisor, you need to resist the temptation and think of the long term. A NO today will help you build trust with the client in the future. The added incentive might help you in the short term, but if the client does not reap the benefits, you may end up losing the client.

Let me illustrate this with an example. Let's say a new automobile company comes in: will you jump on the bandwagon and just buy their product? For instance, you have to buy a four-wheeler. Will you go for an old school, well-established company or a new brand which has just arrived in India? Most people would go for a Maruti or a Hyundai as it is tried and tested. The set brands are familiar amongst the people and hence, they connect. The well-established brands definitely rule the market. Some of them are even pioneers in their respective industries. They are just the best at what they do.

The same is the case for financial products. When we have highly established brands, offering a new product or company should come in only after you have complete knowledge of the product. You should be well-versed with the pros and cons of the product. Only when you gain complete confidence in the product should it be presented to the clients. Experimenting with any product/company should only be chosen when you have full faith in it.

As a financial advisor, it is my moral responsibility to take good care of my client's funds and not play with it just to make a higher revenue for myself. It may come as a shock to you but in the 13 years that I've been in the industry, I've never insisted on selling a new product, nor have I worked with a new company. None of my clients had any exposure to losing money in any scam or defaulter company because I never dared to experiment with my clients' hard-earned money. I see a lot of advisors opting for instant gratification over long-term success; they are the ones who don't survive in the long term.

Also, when there is a new product in the market, they are usually time-bound, meaning their subscription can be taken up only within a limited time period. In such a case, the entire working pattern changes. We have a certain roadmap set for each one of our clients that has to change to accommodate a new offering. We should stick to our roadmap and not adapt to the new offering. These new products will keep coming and going. We will not have the bandwidth to adapt to change all the time. I do not want to end up following the herd just for the heck of it.

Do not go with the flow. These time-bound products attack the advisor with a certain subconscious pressure, which might make you lose focus or deviate from larger business opportunities. Sometimes, when there are only four days left for a new offering to close, there is pressure on the advisor and he may end up missing out on higher priority tasks, which would have reaped him bigger benefits.

The idea is to not get distracted and just stick to your own plan and keep implementing it.

I use certain parameters to filter the products available in the market and then suggest the best ones to my clients which fit their hand like a glove. I work with only the top-notch companies in the financial sector, or any sector for that matter. These companies deliver decent returns, tend to have high settlement ratios, are clear about their offerings, have inspiring and trustworthy leadership, are established brands and have a history to back their claims. There are a lot of companies which will always keep their customers' interests as their priority; their core is based on trust. I'm sure this brings down revenue in the short term, but it will help you in building relationships which will eventually increase your revenues in the long term.

"A NO today will help you build trust with the client in the future."

2.5 THINK, IT'S YOU

"If you don't take care of your customer, your competitor will."

– Bob Hooey

I recently came across a client who had taken a huge hit because of the crash in the stock market. He was frustrated, raging with anger, and abusive towards a certain financial advisor. After deeply scrutinising his portfolio, I realised that he was well within his rights to be furious. His advisor had suggested something radical to him. This is a very usual occurrence in an industry like ours.

There are numerous advisors who take the client's money for granted and just try to push the product that they want to. They do so because these products give them higher commissions or enable them to achieve certain targets. Every suggestion that you make as an advisor should be tailor-made for your client's needs.

One of the common mistakes that advisors make is suggesting an equity-based portfolio to a client who has never invested in anything apart from Fixed Deposits and has a low-risk appetite. The repercussion is when the market crashes the client loses his faith in your suggestions and will end up bad-mouthing you across town. Another classic one is selling a conservative product to a client who has an appetite for higher risk. Selling an equity fund to a client who wants more liquidity, suggesting an endowment plan to a client who is seeking term insurance, selling a multiple-pay structured product to a customer seeking a one-time pay product are commonly made mistakes by advisors. These advisors are making the mistake of placing their commissions above long-term relationship building with the client.

The aim should be to build a long-term relationship with the client by establishing trust and gaining his confidence in your suggestions. The way to achieve this is to understand his needs and then give the best suggestions accordingly. Do not make the mistake of chasing incentives. I know it's important to feed your dogs as well, but think long-term. Try to step into their shoes, think it's for you and see what the best way is so that you can help them achieve whatever they want. Think and scrutinise well if the product you suggest to your client is what you would buy yourself too under the same circumstances. If the answer is yes, go ahead and offer it to your client as well. And if it's a no, you know what to do. You cannot be suggesting a product that you are not comfortable buying. Always note, if your suggestions work and if the client gets the desired results, he will come back to you for more advice. He might even refer his friends and relatives to you. I know that it's the age of digital marketing but nothing works better in marketing than word of mouth. People always give priority to the suggestions of a friend or relative.

There is a simple roadmap that I have derived and usually use to help build long-term relationships with clients. It involves suggesting the best products suitable for them. The aim is to educate them about what suits them the most and to help them make the most out of their hard-earned money. Some basic data that I ascertain from my prospects:

1. The financial status of the client – This cannot be ascertained easily; there's a lot of homework that goes into finding out the net worth of the prospect. Once you have a fair idea of his net worth, decision-making becomes more informed and suggestions become more data driven. You can maybe suggest investments with higher ticket sizes to an HNI and vice versa.

2. Whether the source(s) of income is steady or uncertain? – Some people have fixed rental income, few others are salaried employees: they have sources of steady income, meaning the amount earned on a month-to-month basis is mostly the same. Whereas, on the other side, an entrepreneur's income might be uncertain. It is a possibility that one month he may earn a lot and the next month he may earn peanuts. Is the business seasonal or running throughout the year? This question will again help us to assess the risk appetite better and help in making a more informed suggestion.

3. The tax status of the client – You need to procure the details of which tax slabs the individual/company falls under, what kind of taxes they pay currently, and how much more room they have for tax savings.

4. The financial goals that he is seeking – This will help you to understand the main reason behind the client seeking investment recommendations, which could be his daughter's wedding, his son's education, business expansion, an additional source of income or even just a retirement plan.

5. The time horizon that he is comfortable with – This will help you in determining whether the client is seeking returns right away or if he is ready to wait for a while before the returns start kicking in. Whether the client is trying to put aside some money to expand his business later on. This question needs to be answered in alignment with the financial goals; some clients have unrealistic expectations.

6. The kind of liquidity that would make him sleep at night – This is a very important factor because this helps you to understand the client's goals a little better and in a more specific manner so that you can suggest a portfolio accordingly. For example, a client seeking high liquidity might best be invested in a more liquid product which enables him to withdraw investments any time.

7. The client's appetite for risk – This is again a crucial factor. Rule of thumb, the more the appetite for risk, higher the returns and vice versa. Is the client aggressive or conservative in nature? You might want to suggest an FD to a person seeking low-risk investment, whereas, an equity portfolio may be suggested for an aggressive client seeking higher returns.

Your primary objective behind seeking the above information should be to determine the prospect's goals and make the best recommendation to him based on his requirements. Always remember, the more the information, the more informed the decision. Your recommendation to them should be a balanced product which fulfils all the requirements of your client without compromising on any factor. For instance, keeping only revenue in mind while suggesting a product might at times block the liquidity of a person, which will end up creating restrictions for your client in the future.

It's also a possibility that sometimes prospects might have misunderstood a certain product: the above parameters will help you educate them and explain why you are suggesting a certain product over the other. You need to understand your client's needs, your client's objective, before suggesting a product. You need to get into your client's shoes and check whether the plan suggested by you fits you well or are there any loopholes and room for better suggestions. At the end of the day, the client's happiness and his satisfaction with your services is what is going to put food on your table. You need to put the client's objectives above your greed. Remember, slow and steady always wins the race.

"I know it's the age of digital marketing but nothing works better in marketing than word of mouth."

2.6 SPECULATION KILLS

"Speculation is not knowledge."

– Robert M. Price

I started my career as a stockbroker in 2007. I was at the peak of my youth; thought I was unbeatable and saw enough movies to make me dream big. The market was at a lifetime high in January 2008. All the brokers were having a gala time, enjoying the high incentive cheques and the continuous inflow of investors. Little did we know we had a tsunami coming our way. The great recession hit us in the following months to make our lives miserable. I'd like to think of the recession as a life-altering phase. It taught me important values and success rules that I swear by till today. It drastically changed the way I think of business and the way I do it.

Before the recession, the stockbroking scene was tremendously good. When the markets tumbled down, business volumes came down to 10% of what we usually did. Subsequently, the revenues also came tumbling down. I knew that this crash would bring a lot of unwanted repercussions and cause a lot of irreparable damage. A large pool of my investors used to come into my office and say, "I lost money because of you," or along the lines of, "I lost money in your office." The clients would go around town, badmouthing me and screaming to the whole world about how they lost their hard-earned money by following my advice, or by betting on my suggestions. This brought a huge negative impact on my goodwill as a financial advisor and as a person too. It also had a huge impact on the other products that I was selling at the time. The clients just lost faith in me. I was stressed. I took it to heart and went pondering over this impact night after night. One fine day, I realised that I was doing certain things in the wrong way. I realised that in the game of stockbroking, we are highly focused on short-term customer acquisition rather than playing the long game. The main culprit here was promoting speculation and timing the market.

Speculation is a stock-market term for gambling. Timing the market is a stock-market term for predicting the time in which the money can double, quadruple, etc. I realised that speculation definitely brings volumes in the short term, but it is not insured from the volatility in the market. Whenever there is a huge crash or downfall in the market, the speculators will incur irrecoverable losses. Some players might even end up shutting shop. Every time the market is volatile or there's a big crash in the market, clients tend to leave us and flock to other investments such as procuring land, investing in other businesses, etc. The most impactful repercussion of this downfall on an advisor is to search and acquire new clients, because the older clients have either lost faith or have shut their businesses, or have flocked to other means of investments or a combination of all.

My Eureka moment occurred when I figured out that speculation is helpful in the short term, but ruining me in the long term. There is no scope for long-term growth. My advice here is to discourage speculation and timing the market. There are many clients who do not listen to my advice though. I advise them against speculation, but they still direct me otherwise. I definitely do as I am told but I become blame-proof with such clients. When they lose money, it is one of those "I'd told you" moments for me. Although, I'm not happy with any of my clients losing even a single penny of their hard-earned money. The loss of a client's money is not always in my hands. If a speculative client loses money, I am not to be blamed; but the client looks for somebody to blame and I end up taking the hit. I should be blamed, had I promoted it (which some advisors actively do), but not otherwise.

There's a queue of advisors who promote this practice to acquire short-term clients, make money off them and then dump those clients and search for new clients. But that kind of business has no sustainability; one fine day, your goodwill will go to the dogs. Why create a business model which is speculative in nature and wherein you need to hunt for new clients every day. It is always better to retain the clients year after year as these are the ones who give you business for generations to come.

I have seen financial advisors who speculate in mutual funds, as well as several other products. These advisors invest the money in active funds because of greater revenue and the clients also find it exciting because of the action-packed nature of such investments. But these are not meant for long-term investments and regular returns. Advisors make this mistake of wasting time by working on the same money time and again. They don't realise that if you churn your client's portfolio, you will be unable to grow revenue for your business. The biggest downside to this is the impact on the other pool of products that we sell. Once the client loses faith and loses money at your office, he will damage your goodwill and withdraw his investments from other products suggested by you. You have to realise that by speculation, you are going to lose out on multiple sources of income. The client ends up withdrawing his entire portfolio because you did not warn him about a possible downside to what he was getting into. It takes a long time to build trust, but a minute to destroy it. It is irreparable damage to your brand and never worth it.

Rather, I generally suggest investments which are good enough to last you a lifetime and do not require regular attention. It might not be fun but definitely more profitable; both for me and my clients. I believe in working with new money rather than for the same funds which I have already worked on in the past.

During the 2008 recession, I had clients, big betters, who lost lakhs in one go. They had the appetite for that kind of investment, but nobody likes losing money. My heartbeat went up; I had to go to their office in the evening and collect that money from them. I ached internally to see my clients suffer such losses. I was not able to concentrate on any other business or clients. I was damn stressed for days together to focus on any other thing except that loss. It's not always about business, it's about trust. It hurt even more to realise that my clients lost faith in me. I learned my lesson the hard way.

So, this time when the pandemic hit us, I wasn't one amongst the many who were affected by the downfall in the stock market. When a lot of advisors were scratching their heads out of stress, I was quite laidback and enjoying my family time. So now you must realise that not speculating with your customers' funds will lead to a stress-free business model.

Not that I am suggesting against equity or the like. My only concern remains that it should be handled with a lot of caution. Setting up the right expectations should be your approach towards such products.

Whatever I am today is because of the business that my clients have given me. I try my best to always make it a win-win situation for both my client and myself. So, keep in mind, it might be fun and action-packed, appealing and what not to speculate and time the market, but it's never worth it. Always think of long-term goals.

Suggesting a product which earns you higher commission without paying heed to your client's interests might earn additional revenue but you will miss out on the broader perspective of winning a client forever. Your head will always have to stoop low whenever you happen to have a face-off with the client. Rather, I will suggest you focus on the well-being of the client and protect his best interests to earn a long-term client and revenue. Don't be greedy to earn revenue from a client from Day 1. Instead, practice the art of being patient as this will fetch you much higher revenue in the times ahead.

I'd like to add a small analogy here. When given a choice to eat a chicken or an egg, always go for the egg. If you eat the chicken you will eat well today, but if you eat the egg, you will eat every day.

"I believe in working on new money every time."

2.7 LIVE-IN VS MARRIAGE

"Live-in relationship is like a Limited Liability Partnership (LLP), whereas marriage is a long-term security."

– Unknown

India is changing as a nation. We have opened our minds, come out of religious restrictions and become broad-minded towards our approach to life. As the country is growing, the countrymen are growing too. We are adopting the western culture, taking inspiration from the positives in the western countries and accommodating that in our own country. We are changing for good and moving towards a more democratic way of life. Obviously, we have our bunch of primitive thinkers and life leaders intact, but a decent portion of our population is adapting to changing times. It will take some more time for these kinds of changes to reach the rural sections of our society.

I'd like to harp on one radical change that this western culture has brought to us Indians. I'm sure you have come across this change too. We have a huge infusion of live-in relationships over/before marriage. Adults these days prefer this kind of arrangement over or before a marriage because this involves zero commitment. They don't have to commit; it's like trial and error. They stay together before involving themselves in a long-term commitment (marriage). This arrangement helps them to dip their feet in the waters and see how things work out. Either party has the freedom that if shit goes south, they are free to walk away. This methodology is stress-free, keeps the freedom intact and gives high flexibility.

You must be wondering why I am talking about live-in relationships. What is its relevance to finance? This analogy is highly relevant in our industry. Whenever I'm lost, I flip back to this chapter of my book of knowledge and take inspiration from the above analogy. When recommending a product to a client, I always try to assess his level of commitment. I make it a point to gauge and identify their thought process, their mentality and, most importantly, the level of commitment they are seeking. If you recommend a client who believes in a no-strings-attached relationship to take up a high-level commitment product, most probably he will not. Commitment is motivating for some while freedom ensures power for others.

Let me explain. There are many primitive products available in the market today such as Endowment plans, Bonds, PPF (Public Provident Fund) and NPS (National Pension Scheme). These products have a certain commitment baggage ranging from low to high. You end up investing every year due to the commitment involved and there is less flexibility to exit whenever you feel like. On the contrary, there are highly flexible and zero-commitment products such as mutual funds and fixed deposits. You don't need to put money into them every year and you have the flexibility to exit as and when needed. I always hate to generalise, but there are broad categories of investors. You have a group of primitive investors who are willing to commit and invest in products like traditional policies and PPF. Another group, these are old-school investors but have adapted over time, they would still consider new insurance products. And the last bunch, the bunch with moderately modern thought processes, would probably go for mutual funds or equity.

As an advisor, you also need to identify the investment history of the client and the current portfolio he is holding; dig deep and try to see if there is a pattern that he follows. History will tell you about the past investments that he had made: his appetite for commitment and how it resulted, whether in his favour or not. The current portfolio will tell you, again, his appetite as well as the room left for commitment, if any. These factors will help you to take a more educated and informed decision and recommend investment opportunities accordingly. It's always suggested to have a balanced portfolio; all the eggs in one basket may incur unwanted results.

The objective as an advisor is to make the client come back again and again for advice. You should never look at it as a one-time business transaction. It's always better to think long term. Think of it this way, repeated visits mean repeated income. The roadmap to enable this is to make sure you assess the client's needs correctly, understand the person's appetite too, figure out his level of commitment and then suggest the best product to him. A client's liquidity shouldn't be blocked unnecessarily. It is always advisable to suggest products which give returns without restricting their liquidity. This will fetch him desired results and he will be a client forever. Moreover, you need to have a modern product basket as more and more people are progressing towards equity and mutual funds rather than primitive products. If you keep offering traditional product baskets only, you might lose out on a wide range of clients.

I always believe in one thing: bet on the jockey and not the horse. Make sure you're a damn good jockey to bet on.

"Commitment is motivating for some while freedom ensures power for others."

2.8 ONE-STOP SHOP

"A great department store, easily reached, open at all hours, is more like a good museum of art than any of the museums we have yet established."

– John Cotton Dana

One day, as I was leaving to the office, my wife requested me to drop her off at a department store which was off my route and 3 km away from my residence. I wondered what made her choose that particular store for mere household stuff. I did not question and agreed to drop her. But the curiosity got to me and I started firing my queries mid-way. I mentioned a few shops which were closer to our place, assuming that she was unaware of the same. That is when she explained to me the need of going to that particular department store.

She brought to my notice that her shopping list had all sorts of stuff and not just regular household items. Right from groceries to toiletries, from dusting cloths to exquisite dairy products, she had to buy everything for the following month. The department store is a one-stop solution to fulfil all her requirements. The hassle-free experience made her come all the way. The parking facility available was also quite smooth so I offered to help my wife with her shopping too. When I entered the store, the ambience, amenities and, most importantly, the enormous product basket are what surprised me. I understood my wife's reason behind being a loyal customer of that department store.

In today's fast-paced world, customers look out for this kind of luxury in every industry wherein he gets everything under the same roof without the hassle of running to and fro and also wasting time and effort. The same holds true for our industry too. It is necessary for all financial advisors to keep an extensive product basket to attract clients and retain them too. This will lead to a sizeable amount of business for any advisor.

If my mutual funds client is in need of life insurance and I am unable to provide it, he will certainly go to a different financial advisor for the same. Let us assume that he goes to one Mr Rohit to buy a life insurance policy. Rohit will provide him with the insurance. But does the transaction end there? No. If Rohit is also into mutual funds, he will certainly follow my client and lure him into shifting his entire portfolio from my office to his. If Rohit is a bigger name than me in the financial world or he is more adept than me, then there is a very high probability that my client will shift base there, irrespective of the excellent services that I had been providing. The sole reason is that Rohit provides what I also provide plus insurance. Humans find it hard to be loyal when given different, better options. So choose to become the best option.

Irrespective of your client base, you need to build a set-up which gives a larger-than-life experience. Even with low-income groups, the challenge remains the same. They too want to get a department store kind of experience rather than an individual store encounter. The sole reason behind this is the additional amenities and services provided by a larger store as compared to that of a smaller one.

In today's world of the internet, people have become more aware of their finances. They scrutinise and weigh all the possibilities before reaching a decision. Never underestimate your client on the basis of his bank balance. Nobody wishes to settle for less. You need to be well-equipped with everything even if you cater to low-income groups.

A larger set-up comes in with a lot of advantages too. The revenue that flows in is much higher here because of better pricing and the experience. When customers find a bigger product basket along with an amazing experience, it is hard for them to resist it. They will surely give you more and more business if you give them what they desire.

If any of your products fail, you will always have something else to offer to your client. You will never let him go empty handed. Don't analyse all the products on the revenue front. Some of them might give low revenue but you still need to add them to your basket. This will help you in retention of clients. It is easier for customers to deal with a single financial advisor for multiple products.

Nobody wants to be associated with 10 different people for a similar kind of service.

This set-up is definitely going to cost you a bomb, but you will realise that it is totally worth it in the long run. And if your pockets do not permit it, don't go for it at once. Keep adding products to your basket as and when possible. Gradually, you will have a huge product basket down the line.

"Humans find it hard to be loyal when given different, better options. So be the best option."

2.9 ONE + ONE = 11

"Alone we can do so little, together we can do so much."

– Helen Keller

According to economist Milton Friedman, the main purpose of a business is to maximise profits for its owners. Business revenue is what keeps a business alive. The more the revenue the more the profits. Each and every business works with the hope of making a profit in the end, but only a few make it a measure of success. Your business goals should be set keeping the revenue and ultimate profits in mind. You need to make decisions based on growing profits to achieve business growth in the truest sense.

An individual's objective should be to stick to his goal of earning revenue rather than the path to reach that goal. A financial advisor has many options to earn this revenue and ultimately grow. It could be insurance, mutual funds, bonds, stock broking, deposits, loans, etc. If the path that you have chosen slows your growth or is not working for you, it is best that you change your path. Being rigid only hampers your returns and, in turn, your growth. You will have to be flexible enough to match your client's expectations.

As suggested in the last chapter, a department store kind of set-up is the need of every financial consultant to grow and prosper in the financial service industry. The financial needs may vary from client to client and also from time to time. You should be able to fulfil all these needs under one roof for the convenience of your client and, more importantly, for the growth of your business. But how you will actually do this is the broader concern.

It can be extremely taxing to offer all the financial products and services by you alone. As an individual, you cannot have expertise in all these varied ranges of products. If you are not knowledgeable enough, if you aren't aware of all the products in detail, it will be redundant to offer these products. Instead of helping your business grow, it will put your goodwill at stake. It will make your consultancy questionable. Being the jack of all trades and master of none is not a wise option in our field.

Make the smarter choice if you are willing to grow. You need to collaborate so as to expand and flourish. None of us are as smart as all of us. When you feel you are ready to get other people on board, then start looking out for the experts in our industry. Reach out to specialists of the particular product which you want to add on to your portfolio. And by joining forces with them, you can easily serve your clients without draining all your energy.

Suppose you are into stockbroking and you wish to add mutual funds to your product category. You can avail the licence and get going. Then again, if you want to expand and become an insurance provider too, that is a different subject altogether. This is when the sharp-witted will go in for collaboration. Tie up with an insurance company/broker/agent and serve your client hassle-free.

I have seen many primitive financial advisors still working with the same set of traditional products. They struggle day in and day out, stuck with the same product and trying to make it work. A product that was successful yesterday might not be in demand today. If you stick to it, you will end up compromising on your revenue. So, you should stick to the fact that you need to earn a livelihood for you and your family. Holding on to a product is not going to take you anywhere. You need to learn to accept changes with time.

Many of these primitive agents are immutable by nature. They are an all-or-nothing kind of person. They have a preconceived mindset and they do not bend it for anything. Their notion that they will not do anything unless and until they are capable of it restricts their growth. For instance, they don't want to endorse mutual funds until the licence is in their name. They believe in not selling products that don't give them 100% of the revenue. But what they fail to see and understand is the fact that they are losing out on the larger revenue too by focusing on the smaller part of the revenue that they have to share when they collaborate with others. They forget that their ultimate goal is to earn revenue and not earn revenue only through a particular product/company. Their approach towards this is totally wrong.

I will explain this with the help of an analogy here. Mr Rohit wants to lose weight and become fit. He chooses to diet to shed the extra pounds. After a month, he realises he hasn't been able to follow the diet as expected because of his social and personal obligations. In this case, he will have to change his course of action to lose weight. If he gets rigid on dieting only, he might never be fit again. But if he opts for the gym or other forms of exercise along with dieting, he is sure to get fitter even faster. With multiple practices, he will be able to achieve his goal earlier and better.

One person or company cannot have all the licences under one name. Even huge companies collaborate to speed up their growth and serve their clients in a more fulfilling way. In fact, I have tied up with an insurance service provider from Kolkata to sell insurance in my city. The sole reason behind this was my lack of knowledge and expertise in the same. I wasn't prepared for it. But this particular company holds expertise in insurance and have been adept in their services. They have a very good name in providing competitive quotes and settling claims with ease. Joining hands with them has added a sizeable amount of business to my portfolio. My clients have also benefited as my product basket has widened and they do not need to go knocking on different doors now. Alternatively, if I had taken the licence in my name, I wouldn't have been able to provide such excellent services.

I wouldn't have been so successful if I had thought of doing it all by myself.

When the pandemic hit us, these collaborations with big names also helped and supported their counterparts by providing them online training on how to run the business, irrespective of lockdowns. Their IT backups acted as an added advantage. And the mental support was priceless.

You need to assess your chosen path well. If you realise that your path is not helping you grow, change your course of action immediately. The earlier you do it the more time you save. For instance, when you are in school, the time required for switching from one class to another is a year. If you take two to three years to complete one standard, then it is not considered success. Because, if you keep repeating the same class, it might get quite late by the time you finish school. And your batch mates will get far ahead leaving you behind. Even if you manage to finish school, your higher studies will get delayed too and it will get difficult for you to find a decent job.

The same applies to your business too. Change, as we all know, is the only constant in life. And even the most established brands globally vanished when they chose not to change within the right time frame. If a change is required, it should be done within a stipulated time. Otherwise, it is not considered growth. A reasonable time duration should be enough for you to decide your strategy. You shouldn't hesitate before changing paths as your ultimate goal should be to earn revenue. Done at the right time, everything holds value. Your competitors will go a step ahead of you if you don't change your path at the right time.

A smart businessman always predicts the damage that is about to happen in his business and does everything possible to minimise this damage. And if he manages to do so, he passes with flying colours by winning over time.

There is no downside to collaborating with experts. Your only concern could be the revenue sharing but, as a matter of fact, it shouldn't be a concern at all as even after sharing the revenue, your overall revenue will be much higher. Your alliance with experts now will lead to generations of more revenue. It will harness the best out of the two of you as both of you will bring your best skills to the table and help each other reach heights.

When you are into business, it is difficult to invest a huge amount in IT backup. When you tie up with bigger names, this IT comes as an added advantage. Their software and technology is an added bonus to take your business forward. Marketing your products also gets easier as these big names provide advertisement support too.

Once you make up your mind on collaboration, it is very important to do your research well. A background check is a must to ensure that you are joining with the right people. And once you are sure of your collaboration, don't be hesitant to promote it. Own your collaborations as your strength. These collaborations only add on to your stature. Don't think of them as your weakness. These partnerships will help you achieve your goal better and make your growth smoother.

"An individual's objective should be to stick to his goal of earning revenue rather than the path to reach that goal."

2.10 EXCEL TO MIS-SELL

"History repeats itself is a myth in our industry."

– Unknown

Trust is not just a word. The whole world, to an extent, runs on trust. When you're taking a flight to go from one city to another, you're entrusting the airline, their crew and, most importantly, the pilot to help you take off safely and land you safely. Trust is inevitable. It's not something that can be bought; it's something that has to be earned. It's easier to lose than win it. When trust is combined with selling skills, it's like a magician equipped with his hat. Selling in today's world is damn tricky, but selling in the financial world is trickier.

It's always important to gain two kinds of trust in the financial industry. First, trust in the financial advisor. Second, trust in the product. In my initial days, I used to face a lot of trouble, like any other newbie, with the trust factor. Clients don't want to bet on a newbie, whether it's a new advisor or a new product.

Earlier in this book, we have spoken about a lot of ways at your disposal to gain your clients' trust. When I faced the bottleneck of gaining trust, I reached out to a bunch of company folks and a pool of senior industry men to understand the ways to combat this situation in my favour. I spent a lot of time with them and the most common advice that the majority of them gave was to sell using spreadsheets.

The Spreadsheet typically contains facts and figures and historical data. It highlights an array of products and their returns in the past few years. So, essentially, the advice that I received was to sell based on history or to sell based on historical data and assumptions based on this data. I seemed to be convinced with this proposition and started to ride along right away. I would be lying if I said it didn't work for me. It worked damn well; I was signing up clients at the speed of light; I gained a significant amount of business and started building relationships. We (my clients and I) were like the Titanic, sailing smoothly until we hit the iceberg. The iceberg in the financial industry is none other than the recession. The markets crashed. The entire spreadsheet and its data got reversed. At that time, when my clients asked me for their portfolios, it had become a tough road to walk on. All the data was red. It was a complete downward trend. I was unable to keep up my word.

In spite of me trying any different way to sell the products, clients kept showing me the data. And I totally blame myself for this. I had gotten them accustomed to the spreadsheets by showing it to the clients each time I promoted a product, even before they asked me for it. That's when I started to ponder and realised that something was fundamentally wrong. This wasn't the right way to sell. Clients look out for only those details and features which we choose to highlight. They may easily overlook the points that we choose not to call attention to.

History is never a guarantee for the future. It is not always necessary that what has occurred in the past will reoccur in the future. The entire premise by using Excel to sell was shouldered on the fact that history will repeat itself. Things look quite perfect on a spreadsheet, but the reality isn't so. There are several schemes which have delivered historical returns, but today they aren't delivering the same. Also, there are several schemes that delivered the worst returns in the past but are doing well now. We are in a business where the product isn't in our control. We cannot control the returns on any investment products, nor can we assure claims on any insurance products.

Hence, I advise you to not go about selling based on the USP of a return or a claim. In reality, it isn't even much of a USP: it just cannot be controlled by you. Spreadsheets are a development made to primarily attract and induce confidence within the customers. All the companies are well-trained on this hula hoop. They try their best to hide the negatives and highlight only the positive sides of a product. They go about promoting the benefits and roll the carpet on the negative side of products.

It became redundant for me to use these spreadsheets anymore; I was losing clients faster than the Japanese bullet train. It took me a while to identify the loophole, but better late than never. I'm glad I finally realised my mistake and changed my game.

My new strategy was all about selling myself first. The idea here is to carve a niche for your business and sell in a unique manner.

Let's take a simple example of the Royal Enfield Bullet. When a person goes to buy the Bullet, they are not really bothered about the mileage. This is so because it has been promoted using its masculine build and other features rather than its mileage. They are bothered about how it looks. The way it cruises. The fact that you can ride it even for kilometres together in a single day. And last but not the least, they want to be a part of the cult called Royal Enfield riders. So, what we see here is, Royal Enfield is playing a totally different ball game altogether. They are not competing with the likes of Bajaj or Hero, who focus on the mileage front and so are their clients who check the mileage every time they get their tanks filled. Rather, they are creating their own league. The entire value proposition has changed. They don't use a lot of data to sell their bikes (read mileage). People have a trust in the brand and so they queue up to own it and not because it promotes its records.

I suggest you follow the same strategy. Be unique. Try to offer something that nobody else does. Most importantly, sell yourself. Make sure that the client is not betting his money on the product but on you, on your gut feeling, on your instinct, on your decision-making.

Spreadsheet-selling is good for doing short-term business, but hazardous for long-term relationship building. Use presentations. Use a small but impactful string of words to convince your client. Use your charisma. Link the relevant product to the goals of the client, to their financial needs. Do show them the data but do not make it the basis for selling a product. Try to create the need for a certain product; sometimes, the clients themselves may not know that such a product exists and they might need it.

Eventually, it all boils down to the fact that the client will only come back if he trusts you, otherwise he won't. Make sure you're an advisor worth relying on.

"When trust is combined with selling skills,
it's like a magician equipped with his hat."

2.11 HIT WHEN HOT

"Strike while the iron is hot."

– Unknown

Email marketing has immensely progressed in today's digital world. My inbox is a kind recipient to a whole lot of marketing emails from numerous brands across multiple industries. I am the recipient of no less than 500 emails per day (I'm not exaggerating). I always ignored them like my cold-hearted ex-girlfriend. I usually have a shortage of time, so I always tend to ignore and prioritise other tasks over sitting and reading all the marketing emails.

One fine day, my mobile phone conked and left me digitally handicapped. I was on the lookout to buy a new mobile phone immediately. Co-incidentally, when I fired up my laptop to check my emails, all I could notice was various promotional emails from multiple mobile phone brands. I viewed a few of them to see if I could land some good offers on a new mobile phone. I was able to bookmark a bunch of emails. Some wanted to highlight a new phone that they have launched, some were eager to communicate about the mouth-watering offers on their bestselling phones, and the remainder of them were mostly junk (which I had rightfully ignored).

My point here being, we humans are simply driven by our needs and wants. When you are in need of something, you tend to start noticing it everywhere. You give your time to finding the right product. You research and compare the multiple offerings that are available in the market. Regardless of the medium by which you are being approached, such as emails, phone calls, texts, TV advertisements, Newspaper ads, hoardings, etc., when you do not need that product/service, you are inclined to be ignorant about it. The phenomenon of frequently and co-incidentally coming across the things that we want to buy when we have planned to buy is called selective perception.

The above concept is highly relevant to our industry as well. One of the most important factors in the financial industry is timing. If you try to push a client to buy health insurance when he is not looking for health insurance or if he already has an insurance policy, your requests are going to fall on deaf ears. When the client is on the lookout for a product: that is the right time to approach. He will take your calls, he will pay heed to your emails, in fact, he most probably will have a meeting with you or visit your office. I always suggest, hit the iron with a hammer when the piece of iron is hot, only then will it bend. If you keep hitting the iron when it's cold, it will not change its shape. Similarly, when the client is ready to take up something, go all in, approach from all sides, and you are guaranteed to get his attention and will most likely close the deal. The timing is the most important part.

Now, you may ask, how do I get to know when is a good time? Earlier, this used to be a game of trial and error, but now with this digital adaptation, life has become easier as the dynamics of business has changed. This can simply be done by maintaining a simple database. I'm sure you gather some basic data such as name, mobile number, email ID, location, etc., when you do your homework on the client or before on-boarding a client. All this data works well. Try to gather more data. You need to have constant internal assessments and try to retrieve as much data as possible. It's crucial to have an updated database which enables you to duly follow up with clients as and when required, and try to pitch the most suitable products to them. Be ready with a no nonsense quotation while proposing the particular product.

Let me try to illustrate with an example. When you know the date of birth of a client, you can contact him two months prior to his DOB with a new insurance policy or an upgrade from his current one. There are high chances of him lending an ear to your pitch. Same case in point, if the client already has an insurance policy from a different insurer and if you are able to ascertain his renewal date, then you can again try to approach two months prior to the renewal date and pitch to maybe upgrade his current plan or add on some additional benefits. I can assure you, your words will be heard; there's a good chance he will consider and the probability of you closing the deal will be higher.

I usually make note of the registration number of the cars of my prospects. This helps me to go back and cross reference and help me retrieve data on which insurance he has currently and when the renewal date is. Another crucial chore could be having frequent conversations with your clients. The more the conversations, the more details you are able to extract. Everyone loves talking about themselves or their business. Light a spark and see where the conversation goes. Data extraction will become a smooth process once you have engaged your client in a meaningful conversation.

When the client gives you relevant data like Insurance renewal data, investment portfolio and maturity of deposits/insurances, etc., half the job is done. The fact that he is giving data signifies that he trusts you and is interested in your offerings or probably wants to be boarded by you. Most likely, this practice will also lead your client to expect your call before his renewal date as he gets mentally prepared in the due course of time to give you business. Sometimes, having conversations at a personal level help too. If you get to know that your client's daughter is getting married soon, it's better not to suggest any investment products. He already has a huge upcoming expense.

Data also ensures that you do not make mistakes. In case there has been a mishap in your prospect's family and you are aware about it, it will restrict you from making unwanted calls in times of crisis, thus saving you from unwarranted negative points.

When you have the relevant data, you need to analyse and use it to the best of your ability. In today's date, you have to be data driven; remember, data is the new oil.

"Everyone loves talking about themselves or their business."

2.12 WAIT OR CREATE

"Opportunities are like sunrises. If you wait too long, you miss them."

– William Arthur Ward

All the factors that we have been discussing across this book go hand in hand. There is no one size fits all solution to signing up prospects. It's a simple game of applying what's applicable based on the needs and wants. In today's highly competitive financial market, it is extremely difficult to onboard a new prospect. A back-breaking task that sucks up a lot of time. Often, it so happens that I try my best to on-board a new prospect and fail. There are multiple reasons behind this failure. We need to deeply assess each of the reasons and learn from our mistakes, and see how we can improvise our approach going forward.

There have been instances when it has taken me even a span of more than five to seven years to successfully on-board a prospect. I tried relentlessly, but did not give up. I feel for the folks who give up easily. It takes a lot of grit and effort to chase and sign up a prospect. Ultimately, it's all a part of the cycle. We have to play the Tom-and-Jerry game to win our bread and butter. One of the major reasons that prospects don't look at our faces or shrug us off is because they already are connected with some other advisor. If the prospect is not satisfied with his current advisor, the meal is ready; we just need to add a little salt and pepper and we're done. But, on the contrary, if the prospect is abundantly satisfied with the current advisor's services, we have to strive. The current advisor has taken good care of the prospect. He takes care of all his needs, recommends a solid portfolio that fulfils his goals. He gives a satisfactory service overall. Or maybe he just has a better relationship with the prospect.

Now, to onboard this particular prospect, we have to beat the current advisor at his own game. We are facing a situation wherein the prospect is already satisfied. We need to give him reasons proving that we can do a better job than his current advisor to create opportunities. Or show him where the current advisor is wrong. Broadly, I'd suggest a combination of both.

The first step is to be in constant touch with the prospect. Don't ever let the prospect forget that you exist. Decide a time interval. Annually, biannually or quarterly, that's at your discretion on a case to case basis. Have meetings with the prospect, chit chat. Start with small talk. Discuss about business for a very small duration. Focus more on collecting data rather than selling. Don't plead for business; simply strike a healthy conversation. Be on the lookout for him to bring up finances. Then play your trump card and discuss the products and services you offer.

Gradually, up the game meeting by meeting. You need to have discussions and impress him with your knowledge and skills. When you do this at regular intervals, there's a good probability that the prospect will slowly start opening up to you. You will be able to open new avenues for yourself. He will end up intrinsically gaining confidence in you. He will start sharing details about his portfolio to you. He may talk about certain stocks that he owns, an insurance policy, or perhaps his portfolio of mutual funds.

As a business seeker, the goal is to onboard the prospect. We are seeking business. No financial advisor is 100% correct all the time. It's impossible to be. When you are in constant touch, you will gain insights on the modus operandi and the recommendations of the current advisor. Now is the chance once the groundwork has been laid. It's time to sniff for meat. Look for loopholes. Or rather, look for an opportunity. Scrutinise and hunt for a step from the current advisor that could be passed on as a mistake. Maybe the products suggested are wrong, the infrastructure is not sufficient to handle the business well, lack of technology, maybe the services in case of claim settlement are not good enough, or his products are overpriced. Find some dirt and create an opportunity by coming to the rescue. Rightly put across, "Don't sit at the shore and wait for the waves to wet you. Dive right into the ocean."

Once you've found the opportunity, go full throttle. Grab it. Go in all guns blazing and convince the prospect on how the current advisor is lacking and why it's better to bet on you. There are high chances that the prospect will sign up. So, it is up to you to decide whether to wait for an opportunity or create one.

"It takes a lot of grit and effort to chase and sign up a prospect. Ultimately, it's all a part of the cycle. We have to play the Tom-and-Jerry game to win our bread and butter."

2.13 20 > 80

"Strive for excellence in few things rather than good performance in many."

– Richard Koch

The life of a financial advisor is always a busy one. On most days, we have a lot on our plate. A huge to-do list to comply with. Some folks use planners or perhaps a calendar to plan their day. From meeting the client to meeting Relationship Managers (RMs) from various organisations, getting trained and training our team, transaction punching, documentation, filing, sharing and procuring data, support service, etc. are some of the chores that we have to deal with day in and day out. All these mundane tasks are a part of our business and have to be performed to maintain customer delight. The weighing scale will always point out the above tasks to be equally important. Neither of the tasks can be postponed nor ignored on a daily basis. We need to analyse and prioritise our tasks based on certain metrics.

In my opinion, time is the most important resource at the disposal of human beings. The following concept is one that is applicable to any industry and humans in general, though it is a crucial catalyst in our industry. As a financial advisor, you need to assess the tasks carrying high importance and prioritise them over all others. Automatically, the tasks that help generate significant revenue will become high-priority ones. The microscopic view will exhale one such task which stands above all. Telephonic and physical meetings with clients. Meetings, in our industry, are the most fruitful tasks that help us to generate revenues. Everything else is mostly follow-up or support. The task of following up with the client regularly and seeking an appointment for a meeting is an effort made with the vision to accrue the end result of a meeting. Meetings are where actual conversations happen; they are the core of our business and help us generate significant revenue.

I would like to illustrate this with a simple metaphor with the use of an automobile. A vehicle is a complex tool used for conveyance. Assuming that all the parts of the vehicle are intact, it is ready to take you from the origin to the destination. The most important component required to move the vehicle is fuel. Without fuel, it's a showpiece. All the other parts are important too; any harm to the other parts can be managed to an extent. But the vehicle definitely cannot run without fuel as it is the most important driver. Similarly, in our industry, client meetings are very important. They are the fuel to our business.

Most of us spend time focusing on other tasks and miss out on important ones. If you are spending your time performing other tasks which aren't of high priority, you are restraining your progress. This is a very common trap that most financial advisors fall prey to. Due to poor planning and time management skills, the usual advisor takes maybe one meeting per day, totalling to five to six meetings per week depending on the number of days he works. Considering this as the average, there is a huge room for improvement. I'd suggest you prioritise and try to double this number. So, when you end up doing about 12-15 meetings per week, your business will grow exponentially. The idea is to give the majority of your focus to meeting clients.

Usually, a financial advisor spends about 20% of his time on client meetings which give him 80% of the revenues. Have you ever wondered what your revenue could be if you dedicated 80% of your time to client meetings? I focus on giving 80% of my time to high-priority tasks (client meetings) and 20% of my time to the remaining tasks. This enables constant growth and improves overall revenue generation.

I have been a huge fan of the 80/20 rule. Let's assume you handle the portfolio of 100 clients. The 80/20 rule suggests that your top 20 (tier 1) clients give 80% of your revenues. Logically, it's understood that we should focus more on the tier 1 clients and give them a larger chunk of your time. Then come the next 30 clients (tier 2), who should be prioritised next. They bring in probably 10% of your revenue. And lastly, the remaining 50 clients (tier 3) who bring in the remaining 10% of your revenue. They too deserve your time and attention, but in very small chunks. Or they can even be delegated. If we happen to lose 10 tier-3 clients, it is relatively better than losing even a single tier 1 client. In case a tier 3 client has a probability of turning into a tier 1 client, then you need to keep the focus going, irrespective of the size of business that he is currently giving you. We need to assess the opportunity cost to analyse and prioritise accordingly. I divide my time and attention directly in proportion to revenue generation.

Client's Potential	Business Potential	Priority
Big	Big	Very High
Big	Small	High
Small	Big	Low
Small	Small	Very Low

The 80/20 rule can be applied to your product basket as well. If you have 10 products in your basket, there are probably 2 such products that contribute to 80% of your revenue. Focus on them. New products should also be given a chance but not at the cost of already established products.

We looked at why we should prioritise and the benefits that we can reap. Now we're going to look at how we can enable ourselves to do this. In my experience of 15 years, I've learnt that any task which does not need my continuous intervention or focus can be delegated. I used to receive a lot of calls from financial companies and clients as well. After spending a lot of my time on these calls, I realised that my precious time was being wasted. I decided to forward all the not-so-important calls to my office number. I do not recommend you to ignore calls from clients. Instead, have someone attend the calls and note down important details that need to be communicated to you.

Whenever I receive calls from clients, I try to understand the nature of calls. If it's a probable business opportunity, I do talk. And if it is a service related call, I tend to respond stating that I'm preoccupied with something else and can have someone from my team call them back. This will decrease the number of calls you receive and also increase the time on your plate. Handling this politely is crucial; some clients tend to take this kind of treatment in unforeseen ways, leading to a lash out. Deal with such clients in a more sensitive manner. To efficiently handle these calls and the set of tier 2 and tier 3 clients, you need to have a trained and experienced back-office team.

Delegation is applicable to the major subset of tasks which are not of high priority. For example, dealing with tier 3 clients can be delegated to your back-office team. Selling of the low revenue generating products among your product basket should also be delegated to the in-house team. You should even delegate follow-up calls of tier 2 and tier 3 clients to the in-house team. Any task apart from client meetings, as much as possible, should be delegated.

A mix of the 80/20 rule and delegation can bring about a lot of change in the way you do business. It will help you be mentally free, which is a prerequisite for business planning and effective meetings. Once you have more time at your disposal, along with a free mind, you can bring your game to grow your business.

"In our industry, client meetings are very important. They are the fuel to our business."

2.14 THE MORE THE MERRIER

"No data is clean, but most is useful."

– Dean Abbott

The importance of data collection has been brought to your notice so far on many accounts. But have you wondered where you will store all this data that you collect? Can you remember everything that you hear? Chances are, you won't. It is impossible to keep it safe and secure in your tiny brain which already has so much stored in it. Researchers have found that when it comes to memory, we don't remember things we hear nearly as well as things we see or touch.

Whenever you are communicating with a client via meetings, phone calls or any other means, make sure to carry a notepad and a pen to jot down all the gathered information. You can also click relevant pictures. The collected data needs to be stored and updated somewhere for future use. It is required to have a specific system in place to feed in all the relevant data that you derive from your customers and retrieve it as and when required. For this, you can either have a Customer Relationship Management (CRM) software or an Excel sheet to maintain all the data. If you are not equipped well technologically, then you can very well maintain a hard copy for the same. Your data related work doesn't end here. How to put this data to the best use is the broader perspective. You need to set reminders, accounting for each and every data that you have. The below analogy will help you understand this in a better way.

Whenever I have an early morning flight to catch, I set multiple alarms so as to not miss getting up on time. I set multiple alarms on my mobile phone, my wife's phone too and, just to play safe, I also ask my mom to wake me up early. The purpose of setting off multiple alarms in the morning would only be due to insecurity about not being able to wake up from deep sleep. It is just a matter of precaution so that if I lapse one such call, there is always a second one coming up. And these multiple alarms are set for those tasks that I cannot afford to miss at any cost.

Same concept should be followed in our business. I will explain how. When you have your data in place, you know the renewal dates etc. of your client's policies and investments. Suppose your client's insurance plan is expiring five months later. You need to set a reminder way in advance of the renewal date. And if you don't set this reminder, the amount of effort that you put in to collect the data goes to waste. But think of the time when you are reminded of the said date, it's the perfect time for you to pitch in your proposal to the client and grab the opportunity.

Setting up a reminder is a very important task. There shouldn't just be one single reminder for any work.

Instead, I choose to work on multiple reminder systems in my office and have seen the difference it has brought to my business. I have a CRM software which reminds me of each and every task. Alternatively, I have a physical data bank so that I don't get stuck in case my software crashes. Alongside, I designate each task to at least two employees. This keeps us in check if either I or my team miss out on a particular task. My CRM system also sends out notifications on each of our phones to remind us of the assigned task. So, the more the merrier.

A monthly to-do list is printed and kept on every RM's work station at the beginning of the month. This reminds them on a daily basis of the assigned work. Additionally, a weekly to-do list is written on the soft board and kept in my cabin. These reminders make sure to get the work done on time without even a single job being missed. Hence, I advise you to follow numerous reminder systems. The more the number of reminders, the more the number of follow-ups from your end. Follow-ups are the key to a successful business. Relying on a single alarm might get you to lose the opportunity and, eventually, the client.

Suppose you approach a client with an investment proposal or a product and he tells you his wish to acknowledge it five months later. What will you do now? Will you wait for him to call you or remind you after the said period? Or, do you expect him to remind you once the five months have passed? Of course not. It becomes your responsibility to contact him at that time. And you can only do this if you have a support system to remind you of the same.

Another situation could be when a particular RM is on leave and he has been assigned a task. In such a case, who will be the recipient of the reminder? Make sure there is a process which redirects the reminder either to you or any of your support team members.

I have a reminder system which has been programmed with tasks which are to be done several years from now. If I have a client who has been insured by some other advisor and the policy will mature in say 2030, I will add the details to my CRM and set a reminder for 2029 to plan the reinvestment of his maturity amount as it is a lucrative business opportunity for me. This alarm in 2029 will help me follow up with the client and get business out of him.

The more data we collect and the more reminders we set, the more business we will do. You will have multiple reminders every single day. This will lead to your to-do list being full on a regular basis. Imagine if you are able to build a database of 1000 clients, leading to 2000 business opportunities in a year. And you are able to convert even 60% of the clients, i.e., 1200 leads in a year, which roughly averages to four opportunities daily. Imagine the growth in your business. This way, you will not have to sit idle wasting your valuable time looking for business opportunities. You will always have some client or the other to focus upon. And if this continues for the second year too, you will have 4000 business opportunities the next year. If this is followed year after year, then your business is sure to grow manifold.

All this is possible only when there is a reminder system in place which keeps knocking you every moment and doesn't let you sit idle. The more the opportunities, there are increased number of alarms in your system, ultimately leading to exponential business for your company.

"The more data we collect and the more reminders we set, the more business we will do."

2.15 LOST! NOT AGAIN

"Everything you have ever wanted is on the other side of fear."

– George Addair

Have you faced loss of a business opportunity to a competitor? Have you ever been rejected because of your incapability to meet a client's expectations? Was your not-so-good relationship with the client the reason for lost business? Don't let the fear of a lost business opportunity get to you. I have experienced all the above scenarios and more while dealing with clients. Even the best financial advisors go through this at some point or the other. And it must have surely happened with you too. You must wonder what exactly went wrong when you thought all you did was right. You did your homework well, went on to build a strong rapport and must also have prepared a top-notch proposal. In the end, you still had to hear a 'no.' "NO!!" It's never fun to lose a business opportunity, but how you handle these losses can make or break you. What do you do in such situations?

Don't let a 'no' from a prospective client get you off the track. Don't let it happen again. Use it as a learning opportunity. I have closed deals with unexpected clients on more than one occasion. The primary objective in such a situation should be to figure out what actually went wrong. The answer lies within you. You need to assess well what went wrong where. But even before this, you need to handle the client meeting well. In case you happen to lose business in the client meeting, how are you supposed to end that meeting? Definitely not on a bitter note for either of you. It should always close on a positive note, at least from your end. You can end it with a, "Sir, we will try again next year," line or maybe a, "We will give you a better quotation next time," promise. If you do not do this, it will be very difficult to re-approach the client. You also need to keep following up with the client instead of choosing to take a break. Or else, it will become impossible to work with the client in future. Don't assume that after a lost business opportunity from a particular client, he will never do business with you again. Let the future decide that. Your job is to leave the conversation open-ended so that there is no hesitation from either end to do business together in times to come.

Self-assessment should begin now. When you know your mistakes and own them too, it works to the best of your advantage. You know the client in and out. You know whether it was the pricing that didn't work or the relationship with the client that created the loophole. You know who the competitor you lost the game to was. You are well aware of your shortcomings. Now act upon them and turn them to the best of your knowledge. Work hard on your weak points. Make them strong enough to turn the tables around and make them your strengths rather than your flaws. Be sure to grab the opportunity next time at any cost. You also have enough data on the client to inform you about the right time to hit the iron rod. The data that you have collected in the past will act as your staircase to approach the client in future. Keep in touch with the client on regular intervals. Follow up until you succeed.

The below said situation should be explanatory enough. Suppose you lost Mr Rohit's business due to better timing of your competitor and also his closer bond with him. You realise where you lacked. You now have a full year to work on Mr Rohit's profile and offer him a better deal next time. Put in all your effort to establish a warm and healthy relationship with Mr Rohit in the following year. Work on his portfolio well and prepare a proposal which he will not be able to refuse. If you do your homework well, Mr Rohit is sure to consider you again in the coming years.

Losing a business opportunity should not result in loss of hope too. You are not the one who gets to decide if the client gives you business or not. Your job is to keep following up. Lost business this year is an easier opportunity next year. It is as good as half the job done. Own up your mistakes and learn from them. You will grow bigger and better.

"Follow up until you succeed."

2.16 WHAT ABOUT TOMORROW?

"If your business comes from relationships, relationships should be your business."

– Doug Ales

Forever is a long time. How do you make your business last forever? How do you model it such that it builds forever relationships and earns you loyal customers for generations to come? Many business experts might say, "Beat the competition." But, I believe it is much more than that. The oldest existing advisors didn't get where they are by simply beating the competition. The best way to reach the next level of wealth is not only to build a business, but to make your business last forever.

In our industry, many times it so happens that we lose a very old client all of a sudden and the reason behind this goes unidentified. This is very common yet disheartening. In most cases, the reason turns out to be your relationship with the client. Let us talk about a business family. There are many members who belong to a huge joint business family, but the decision–maker is only one. It could be the grandfather of the family or the eldest amongst his sons. The decision-maker generally is just one person, irrespective of the size of a family.

If your aim is to form a long-term relationship with a business family, you need to have a bond with all the generations of the family and not only the torch bearer. If there are three generations in the family, you should be familiar and friendly with all three, which includes the grandfather, father and also the son. In case the father is the decision-maker and you are on good terms only with him, the grandfather might influence him to consult a different advisor. And if you are not friendly with the son, a few years later when he starts handling the finances on his father's behalf, he will reach out to people who are close to him and not you. So, now is the time when you need to work on relationship building with all the generations.

A classic case is also that of multiple siblings working in the same firm. Generally, the finances are managed by just one of the siblings and not all of them. If you keep meeting and greeting only this particular sibling, what will happen tomorrow when these siblings part ways? Your bond with others will never grow or even form. And when they reach a point of separation, which is inevitable, the other siblings will not be keen on your financial advice anymore. You will lose out on those business opportunities which would otherwise easily be on your plate had you paid attention to each of the siblings and treated them equally. This will lead you to lose more than half of your existing business too.

I follow this policy of maintaining healthy relationships with each member of a family mandatorily.

Whenever I go to a client's office, I make sure to meet the decision-maker at last. I first head towards the cabin of other members and meet them personally each time I visit their office. I engage in small talk and go on to share their portfolio details with them individually. This helps me build a cordial relationship with them, which is sure to last for generations to come. If I don't make an effort to meet the other members, they are sure to think of me as the decision-maker's man. They will build a wrong impression of me in their minds and start resenting me and try to replace me with their choice of financial advisor. It is always advisable to be everyone's favourite and not just favoured by one. This also holds true for companies with multiple directors, as well as in case of working couples.

Forming a healthy relationship with the older generation is a matter of respect and attitude. But when the younger generation steps in, you need to be more than just friendly. You need to upgrade yourself technologically to keep pace with the rising generation. Keep yourself updated and informed as they are ever evolving. Try establishing an informal relationship with them by striking a conversation whenever they bump into you. Create an aura which makes them look up to you and idealise you. Maintain a bond with them from the early days and see it flourishing over the years and giving you its fruit in the future.

To make a business last forever, it is not simply enough to build relationships with all the generations of your client. To do business with all the upcoming generations, your business should also be such that it lasts for your family's generations to come.

Family businesses are the primary form of business all over the world, yet very few of them are able to last for a second generation, let alone a third generation. Why does it happen so? The fault lies in the business model. Hence, I want to build a model which benefits upcoming generations. I aspire to create a business which provides me with a handsome salary even after my retirement. And if my children end up pursuing something other than financial advising, they should be able to reap the profits of the business their father had laid the foundation of. My vision is to build a business for generation after generation.

This will happen only when you have created a business model which can run on auto mode and function without you even when you are unavailable. Thisis not possible in a day or two but, with continuous effort and a rock-solid model, you can definitely make your business on autopilot mode. Only when you are able to achieve this, your business will function for generations and even after you are gone.

Creating a brand name for yourself and your company is what does wonders. A brand name stays forever, for as long as you wish to do business in that name, for many generations to come. I would suggest you to not keep the company in your name. If you do so, then your successor might not want to continue in your name and might want to change it. Additional effort will have to be put in from his end to earn goodwill for himself with a new name. But if the company has a unique name, he can easily carry it forward without any hesitation.

With passing years, you need to grow your business too. You cannot expect yourself to sit at the same stature for years and yet expect your business to grow and live for generations. You have to keep expanding yourself year after year if you want to serve the future generations. You should plan and work hard every day to be the largest player in your territory. You have to be prepared for any threat that might appear in the form of national players. In fact, these national players should consider you a threat before entering your territory and should be well aware of your credibility. Only this will help you survive the big names and let your business flourish for generations to come.

"The best way to reach the next level of wealth is not only to build a business, but to make your business last forever."

2.17 PLAN B

"The most successful people are those who are good at plan B."

– James A. Yorke

Things don't always go as planned. They tend to bend and go sideways many times no matter how well you plan for them.

You have a whole day planned out when something unexpected comes up. You didn't see it coming. These situations will and always do happen. What do you do in such situations? This is why PLAN B. Always a PLAN B. Just in case.

Most certainly you don't. A lot of people are so far behind on Plan A, i.e. their original plan, such that they never give themselves time to think about a Plan B. Being prepared for the unknown is certainly difficult. But the point is to be prepared enough and planned out so that you can adapt to unforeseen circumstances.

I am a businessman who believes in foresight. I plan everything well in advance and I make sure to have a contingency plan in place. Right from planning my day, my regular routine and my business format, I chalk out every small move that I am to make.

On many occasions, it so happens that a client cancels the meeting due to some reasons. What are you supposed to do in such a situation? You either waste that time and crib about it or have an alternate plan in place to make constructive use of the said time. Or you have a meeting scheduled with a client and you propose a particular product. What will you do if he rejects your product proposal in the first five minutes of the meeting? Will you come back empty-handed? Would this be a smart move? Definitely a big no. The ideal move would be to carry an alternate product basket and be ready with the specifications and quotations for it as well. This way, you will not waste that one important client meeting which you were looking forward to for days.

Many of the financial advisors depend on only one product or one company for their revenues. What if the product fails or the company crashes? What if the product which generates the maximum revenue for you sees a complete downside? The client which gives you a good share of business suddenly locates to a different city or chooses to change his financial advisor. What will you do in any of the above mentioned scenarios? How will you act upon changing circumstances? This is where Plan B comes in. A contingency plan is a must for all things that bring revenue for your business.

You need to always have a back-up for everything. For instance, I have subscribed to three internet providers for my office. Just in case one doesn't work or is slow, my office work shouldn't take a back seat. Another classic case is when an employee quits his job without prior notice. In that case, I always have an employee ready to fill in his position. I make sure to have an extra employee trained and ready to take the position of anybody who holds important managerial and operational positions and leaves without prior notice.

When you have a Plan B, all your resources and time are utilised to the best of your ability. It's important for you to understand that ideally you are going to do 'X,' but if that fails, you need to be ready and make sure that 'Y' happens. This level of preparedness is required to become a successful financial advisor.

Apart from being able to adapt and re-route, having a Plan B also has a lot of other advantages. It lets you consider alternatives. When you are on the lookout for Plan B, you tend to get so many other alternate options to consider which might even be better than your first option. Plan B lets you take advantage of the down time. Suppose your client keeps you waiting longer than expected, what would you do in that time? Utilise it or sit idle and waste it? That is when Plan B comes into use and helps you make constructive use of the extra time. The most important benefit is that it reduces stress and keeps you sane even in situations that would otherwise create panic.

Plan B is sure to cost you a little over the regular expenditure but, in the end, you will realise its worth and also know that it gives you more than it takes. Always have a Plan B and you are sure to make optimum utilisation of your resources at disposal.

"A lot of people are so far behind on Plan A, i.e., their original plan, such that they never give themselves time to think about a Plan B."

3. GRAB THE EYEBALLS

"You can't sell anything if you can't tell anything."

– Beth Comstock

3.1 SPECIFIC IS TERRIFIC

"Be personal. Be relevant. Be specific."

– Seth Godin

Marketing is defined as the process of getting people interested in your product or service. Marketing pertains to all aspects of a business and is present in all stages of business, from beginning to end. It is the connection between the products and the clients. Yet, it is the most complicated term in business. A well-planned and strategised marketing can take any business to heights. And just like any other business, our business also requires a proper marketing plan to achieve its goals.

The only difference lies in the way we market our products. This is because the nature of the products that we deal in is quite different from that of other businesses. Also, the client base we cater to is totally different. Any Tom, Dick and Harry will not be your client. So, it is very important to keep these aspects in mind while planning your marketing strategy.

As discussed earlier, you need to first identify your target audience and your marketing strategy should be specific towards it. This is so because if you go in for mass marketing, it will lead you nowhere. It might reach thousands of people but might not even be close to your actual client base. No random stranger has ever entered my office and asked for an insurance policy or discussed mutual funds. In my work span of 15 years, there has never been a single client who has not been known to me. This financial advising business runs solely on relations and trust.

Print media, like newspaper and TV ads, hoardings, etc. are quite expensive and might not prove to be as useful for you. Rather, shoot your target audience with emails and WhatsApp messages to garner attention. The point is, you don't need to be visible to everyone. Instead, work on a marketing plan which makes sure that your target audience finds you everywhere. Focus on this small group of people and channel all your energy and resources towards them to benefit the most.

It is perfectly okay if the rest of the world doesn't know your business. What's more important is that your target audience should not forget your business.

So, it is very important for you to identify your target audience, build a relationship to lay the foundation for the trust factor and then pitch in your marketing. Marketing your products to a specific identified client base is the key to success for all financial advisors.

"Focus on this small group of people and channel all your energy and resources towards them to benefit the most."

3.2 EDUCATE TO SELL

"What separates good content from great content is a willingness to take risks and push the envelope."

– Brian Halligan

Today's clients live a highly digital life and are well aware of the market around them. They don't have to and will not buy a product unless they are totally satisfied with it. Furthermore, today's consumer won't do business with people they don't trust. They need to be assured that they are placing their finances in the hands of the right financial advisor who has their best interests in mind. This is where education-based marketing plays a major role. Education-based marketing shares complete knowledge and understanding of the products and the company with the purpose of building trust. This helps in reaping the profits of marketing in the truest sense. Don't market just for the heck of it. Market to target your clientele and benefit from it. Result-based marketing is what actually serves the purpose.

Educational marketing is the direct opposite of traditional marketing, which focuses on selling-based messages. When informational content is shared and important information and facts are put forward, customers do pay attention as it guides them to make good buying decisions.

The financial services industry has a huge crunch of people who take the education-based approach. They fail to understand that traditional marketing no longer attracts a consumer and doesn't help at all in turning him into a customer. There is a huge gap between consumer understanding and the financial advisor. And this void needs to be filled in through information, education and knowledge about the product and the company on the whole. Their creatives have a lot of product details that are unimportant to be shared in creatives. Just sales-driven marketing is not enough.

You need to be very careful while imparting this knowledge too. Be selective in the content that you use. Posting anything and everything in the name of educational marketing is of no use. People generally send a social media creative to wish their clients, which is directed towards sales on special occasions. As a consumer, when I receive such creatives like this I get annoyed and irritated. Direct sales pitch is repulsive and does more damage than repair. I mostly block such numbers.

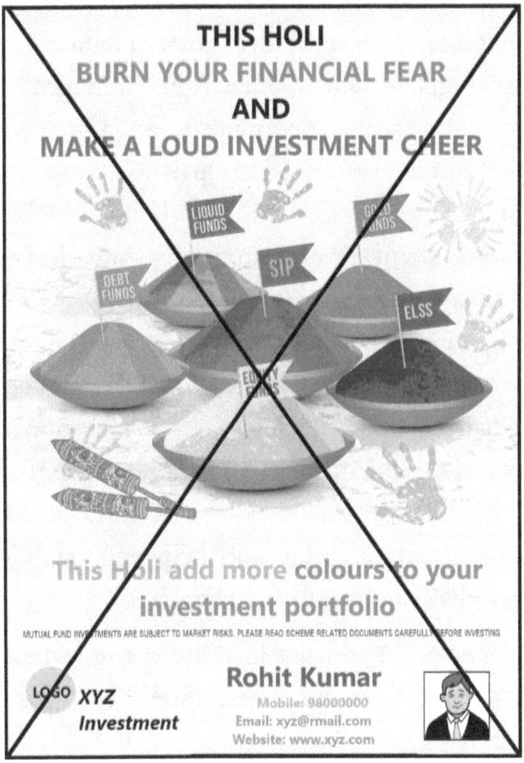

Having an educational presence in the market and building your consumer relationships on the same lines are important in today's business circle and this is applicable to all types of businesses and services. You should work out innovative ways to keep educating your existing clients as well as potential customer base. This will help you build trust over them because they will rely on your content for problem-solving techniques and will also look out for ways to achieve their goals.

You need to identify the touch points of your clients and customer base at large. These include publicity, advertisements, emails, WhatsApp messages, website content, blogs, social media posts, etc. Once you have identified these, you need to pass on your messages through each of these mediums. Being visible in the eyes of your client is very important. And this visibility should always add value to your company. As I believe, out of sight is also out of mind. So you need to constantly approach them in more ways than one. If you keep them posted twice weekly, i.e. eight posts per month, then keep only a couple of posts as sales promotion and rest should be focused on imparting education. This will increase your brand value and help you establish top-notch goodwill amongst your clients.

Another point to keep in mind is the format of the template that you create. There should be a customised template with your brand name on it. This template should be used in each and every message that you send to your clients, irrespective of the medium. This will

Don't Wait To Start Saving, Take Action Today | Deeva Ventures Pvt Ltd...
www.deevaventures.com

Don't wait To start saving, Take action today

Click her to read the full article.

https://www.deevaventures.com/dont-wait-to-start-saving-take-action-today/

Reply **STOP** to discontinue.

Save this number in your contacts to activate link.

INVESTMENT | LOAN | INSURANCE

create your brand identity amongst your clients and they will recognise your posts even before reading them.

Your templates should be accompanied with some educational content so that it lures the receiver into opening it. Nowadays, nobody prefers to download unnecessary images and spam their inboxes. The better idea is to make the text attractive and informative enough that it urges the reader to download the image too.

During occasions, I would suggest you wish your clients well in advance so that your wishes don't get lost amongst the herd of other messages that are sent out by one and all. As a matter of fact, I have consciously chosen to not send out creatives on festivals and occasions. This saves my team's time and efforts, which would otherwise

Varanasi's No 1 Financial Market Place | Deeva Ventures Pvt Ltd | Introduction
We help investors manage their Wealth, by
youtube.com

Dear **Sir,**

We expertise in helping investors manage their **Wealth**, by providing disciplined advisory on **Portfolio Management, Risk Management & Debt Management.**

Click here to know more about us.
https://youtu.be/uB-Ub8obf0Q

Kindly save my contact card in your phone.

Regards,
Garvit Chaharia
Deeva Ventures Pvt Ltd

www.deevaventures.com

INVESTMENT | LOAN | INSURANCE

Garvit Chaharia | Deeva Ventures Pvt Ltd

Message   Add contact

be wasted as no one reads any of the messages sent out on these days. Instead, I choose to add a pop-up to my website and mobile application, which wishes my viewers whenever they visit us. This way I don't spam my clients.

Also, I make sure to introduce the mobile number to my clients which I use for marketing purposes. This helps in my messages being delivered as the number is already saved on my client's phone.

There is a very thin line between spamming and marketing and you need to understand the difference between the two. We are here to market and educate our readers and not spam their inboxes and earn their ire in return.

Build on content that garners responses for you. You need to do a survey to find out what your clients think and what they are in need of. Accordingly, your content should have an engaging title and it should be built around your clients' challenges, problems, goals, etc. It should make them aware about the various financial products and their merits and demerits. This will enable better decision making. Add value to your clients and prospects and they in return will add value to your business.

Your content should also include a lot of information about the workings of your company. We, as financial advisors, review our client's portfolio every three to six months. A lot of time and effort is invested from our end on each client's portfolio. This needs to be communicated to them through letters or emails, which will strengthen your client's trust in you.

On many occasions, we are honoured by the asset management companies (AMCs)/Insurance companies for the hard work that we put into our business. This should also be brought to notice through messages and posts.

In my office, we celebrate a lot of festivals and occasions with our team. I make sure to capture these moments and create content out of them.

Sharing all these helps in building your brand. This doesn't pitch in sales for sure, but it does garner views and, in turn, makes a space in the minds of the clients.

Your role doesn't end here. Now, when you have created enough content and have started posting them, you are bound to receive responses in the form of emojis, comments, etc. Every response that you receive is a prospective business opportunity. Consider every response as the client's interest in your content. Now, it is your responsibility to turn this interest into business. You need to be spontaneous in your replies before the client changes his mind. You need to closely monitor each response and look at it as a lead. Furthermore, you have to work towards closing the business deal with the prospective client. If you don't have a system in place to monitor these leads and close them, your entire effort and resource of putting up a post goes wasted. Not being active in responding might also create a negative impact in the minds of clients and bring in a bad word for you and your company. The client might feel ignored and neglected, which is not really good for you and your company.

Hence, focus and reply on education-based marketing to gain leads, and work towards turning these into business.

"We are here to market and educate our readers and not spam their inboxes and earn their ire in return."

3.3 TICKET TO "THE GAME"

"No matter what your age is, everyone loves being pampered on their birthdays."

Birthdays are a special time of the year. They give everyone a chance to feel exceptional and loved. You are definitely growing older, but also wiser. No matter what your age is, everyone loves being pampered on their birthdays. They are a cause of celebration and a great chance to show someone how important they are to you. This holds true for clients as well.

As mentioned earlier, I suggest creating a data bank for all your clients and prospects too with their birth dates for records. This is an important day for your client and so for you. It is an opportunity for you to wish your client on his special day. When you make a phone call to him or send him an email or maybe a gift, he remembers you as he feels good about it. This is what makes birthdays a unique marketing gimmick. Wishing him is certainly going to create a good impression about you in the minds of your client, but sending him a physical gift along with a handwritten letter to add a personalised touch can be a big win for you over your client. Practice this for three to four years religiously and see your prospect turn into your client without fail. This will help in creating stronger relationships with your clients. After all, who doesn't like to be pampered and who doesn't hold a soft corner for the person who makes you feel pampered?

Choice of gift is another important aspect in this marketing strategy. It is not about the cost of the gift. It doesn't necessarily have to be very expensive but it needs to be appealing enough for the client to take it home. Make sure to never turn a birthday gift into a marketing object. Don't choose a stationery article like a pen stand or calendar etc. as that will lie on his office table. And if at all it is loaded with your brand's logo, accept that it will go into waste for sure. Nobody is going to use anything that endorses your brand in his office. Pitching in sales on special occasions should be avoided as it creates negativity to a certain extent. So choose wisely.

One year, I chose to send a cookie box to all my clients and prospects on their birthdays. The idea behind it was, sending an edible gift makes them relish it with their family members or office team. And whenever this happens, they are bound to talk about me and my company. How you send the gift is important too. A very small logo on the packaging is enough to create an impact on the client. So make sure to choose the right gift which hits your client and makes him remember it for days. And also pay attention to the packaging details. Even outstation clients are sent gifts via courier facility.

This takes them by surprise and they call back delightedly to thank me for the gesture.

There should be an automated system in place to maintain the data and inform the concerned team about a client's or a prospective customer's birthday. You will not want to miss out on any opportunity with any of the clients. Delegate this work to one of the subordinates as you have much more on your plate already.

Be sure to not go with the gift yourself. This will bring down your value in the eyes of your client. He might think that you are a one-man army. Or he might even place himself in a much higher position than you. To let go of such thoughts, you need to have someone who takes care of the birthday gift deliveries. I generally send the RM of the particular client to present the gift to the client. This helps the RM initiate a small conversation with the client and in turn strengthen their relationship. In case of prospective clients, I delegate it to the RM who would look into the client's portfolio in future. Try not to send the gift through a peon or a driver as he will not be able to strike any conversation with the client. The main purpose of this activity is not to deliver the gift but to build a strong relationship with the client, which would in turn help the RMs to fix up a meeting.

For every little thing, experience is what matters the most. My team and I try to make this special day a joyful and memorable one for our clients. We start by sending a text message to the client, wishing him on his birthday and informing him to expect a surprise which would be delivered by one of our executives. We also send a contact card of the particular executive so that the client receives his call at one go, and make it a hassle-free experience for the client. And I too wish the client without fail either by message or phone call from my personal number to add the personalised touch to the said practice. All this makes the client remember me and my team for making his day a beautiful one.

Follow-up process to this master marketing activity is of utmost importance. You need to set up a reminder for 30-40 days after the birthday to call up the client. This is to make a random call and start a conversation with the client. He will definitely speak to you as the memories of his birthday will be fresh in his mind. This will help you fix an appointment with the client and grab that as a business opportunity. A small gift from your end is the ticket to a meeting with your client which was otherwise a little difficult to set up.

Dear **Rohit** Sir,

Greetings!!!

Deeva Ventures wishes you a very **Happy Birthday.**

We wish you an amazing year ahead that starts with a huge celebration and ends with you accomplishing all your personal and professional goals.

Keep shining!! Keep smiling!!

Our representative **Mohit Kumar** will be arriving with a **surprise** to make your day more special.

Kindly guide him with your address. Please expect his call at any moment.

His contact card is attached below.

Thanks & Regards

Mohit Kumar | Deeva Venture Pvt Ltd

Message | Add contact

In case of grievance with a client during the year, this strategy helps to mend that fallout. It nullifies the grudge that the client might have against you. Also, in the case of ex-clients, this activity helps in recreating the bond and retention of the same.

I highly recommend this over and above all other marketing ideas. I might, at some point of time, stop any of my marketing activities due to lack of funds or resources but definitely not this. I have been following this marketing strategy for three to four years now and it has proved to be a jackpot for me and my company. I will not deny the fact that it is an expensive marketing strategy but it is worth the investment. For the existing clients, it makes them feel pampered and important when their service provider goes an extra step to make their day special. And in case of prospective clients, the birthday wishes and greetings make them come around in a couple of years. This strategy of mine has never failed to amaze me and benefit me.

"Client birthdays are a unique marketing gimmick."

3.4 A BRAND IS FOREVER

"A brand for a company is like a reputation for a person. You earn a reputation by trying to do hard things well."

– Jeff Bezos

Branding, by definition, is a marketing practice in which a company creates a name, symbol or design that is easily identifiable as belonging to the company. A brand is simply the answer to who you are and what you can do. A brand helps to identify a product (in our case, a company) and distinguish it from competitors. It tells the consumers about your offerings and helps them make an informed choice. Your brand is built to be a representation of how you wish to be perceived by your target audience.

In the financial business, there are many national level players who you are competing with day in and day out. These are big names which are a threat to advisors like us. So, for us, branding is all the more important. To compete with them, you need to establish your own brand in your business territory. When you create a brand equivalent to that of a domestic advisor in your territory, a local person will mostly prefer you over a national player. The familiarity with you and your brand will strengthen your stake over the local market. Also, the personalised, hassle-free services that you would provide without the involvement of long queues in customer care are additional advantages for the consumers.

Brand is something that cannot be created overnight. You need to work on it right from the start and create a strong brand which grows with you and your company. There are many aspects to it like advertising, customer service, promotional merchandise, reputation building and logo. All these areas need to be in sync and work uniquely towards one particular objective of creating an attention-grabbing professional brand.

According to Bill Gates, "If your business is not on the internet, then your business will be out of business." An impressive website is a must have in today's business world. An email ID on your company's domain does wonders. When you get your business online, your company arrives on a bigger platform. The client doesn't know who is behind the company while a digital sale is made. It really doesn't matter how big or small an advisor you are, what matters is your digital representation. If you invest and work hard on the technology, you can get any client without worrying about your stature or infrastructure.

I thoroughly believe in this philosophy and have tried to bring a lot of changes in my company accordingly.

I, along with my team, have worked close to 15 years, bit by bit, to create the brand that we are today.

Information Technology has played a great role in creating a brand for my company. To start with, we have an automated IVR system to track all our business calls and keeps our office open 24*7. This ensures personalised experience to each of our clients along with customised welcome greetings and reduced wait time.

Gradually, we have progressed to a personal mobile application which helps us be available on the tip of our customers' mobile phones. The mobile application has let us an entry into the daily lives of our clients by always being in close sight. Clients remember my company each time they scroll through their phones. Thanks to my company's mobile application which is installed on their devices.

I have developed a dress code for my team members which distinguish them as a brand. They are given an ID card as well, which completes their look. All the team members have their personal visiting cards and they all follow a uniform email signature for all their official mails. All the stationery and coffee mugs used in my office have my brand name on them.

Branding is a very important feature for any business. Branding is what gives you a reputation and, ultimately, a future. It has an overall impact on your company and not just sales. A brand helps you connect with your consumers at an emotional level. When you are a known brand and have a good brand value attached to your company, your consumers feel happy to be associated with you and will want to engage with you repeatedly.

A good brand makes it easy to grab referrals. Everyone wishes to work with a trusted brand. Your brand's positive impression will automatically pull in customers through word of mouth. Customers go for a bigger brand name rather than the person involved. Even your employees will be more satisfied with their job if you have a recognised brand. They will be proud of their workplace and will enjoy their work to the fullest.

Branding also brings in the trust factor amongst the clients. They feel more confident to give you business if you are an established brand. If you wish to work beyond your geographical location and enjoy the broader perspective, branding is indispensable. This is what helps you enter the bigger market and establishes a client base for you.

Another aspect that I would like to draw attention to is your brand name. As suggested earlier, you should never have your company's name after your name. If your company's name is after your name, clients will start to associate you with your company. They will always want you to be available for every little thing. But creating a unique brand will help the business run on auto mode and clients will be satisfied enough to work with your brand, irrespective of your availability.

Also, after you are gone, people might forget your company. The association might end if the brand is in your name. But if done otherwise, a unique brand name will ensure people are on the lookout for your brand and not you.

Having a brand ambassador for your business is a smart move as when a person endorses your company, he brings in a positive light on the company. He helps increase the brand awareness and, hence, boosts sales. As growing entrepreneurs, we cannot manage the funds required for hiring a celebrity to endorse a brand. So, for us, our loyal clients are our brand ambassadors. They are the most satisfied clients of our entire base. When this segment of people is happy with our work, they turn into our brand ambassadors automatically. They start to endorse our brand and us through word of mouth. And the type of business we will receive in return will be enormous.

Your job is to work extensively on your top clients and cater to them with the best services possible. Nurture them and serve them to the best of your ability. This will lead them to bring in new clients into your business and help it grow manifold. When your existing clients get you new ones, they will be of the same stature as your old ones. And these clients will enter with an already established trust in your company. If your HNI clients manage to bring in clients for you, they will mostly turn out to be HNI too. So, channel your efforts and work on your top clients to get more and more such clients. This will only increase the number of brand ambassadors you create over time. And testimonials from these clients in the form of videos and write-ups always prove to be an added boon.

Branding, as perceived, is not a very expensive affair all the time. When planned smartly, it can be light on the pocket. One step at a time is the trick to strategise and implement branding effectively.

Your branding strategy should be such that it ropes in new customers every day and helps to uplift your brand value. It should help in the process of creating a strong, positive perception of the company. It needs to actively shape your brand, keeping a consistent theme throughout all marketing communications.

"When you create a brand equivalent to that of a domestic advisor in your territory, a local person will mostly prefer you over a national player."

4. GOOD TO GREAT

"Growth does not come with a single action. It is the consequence of persistence, courage and hard work."

– Unknown

4.1 RENT IT OUT

"Growth requires you to be flexible."

– Unknown

A lot of factors need to be taken into account when you are a self-employed person. From planning the business model to marketing to employee selection, the list is endless. But the most crucial decision which requires you to take a call is whether to rent or to buy your office space. Most financial advisors and business owners look into the potential to build equity in a property while wanting to buy an office space. They eye it as a good long-term investment as generally properties appreciate in value over time. It is quite lucrative to own your own space.

A lot of people take pride in it. But, what they should understand is to keep the business and investments separate. They can buy an estate when they want to invest but they should invest in the business when they want to expand. Clubbing both might restrict your business growth.

I advise on never owning one's workspace. Renting an office space gives you maximum flexibility. You aren't bound by the location or the square footage of the area. It requires minimum maintenance as compared to owning the property, which involves a much higher maintenance cost.

Many advisors choose to work from the comfort of their homes for the sole reason of excluding the monthly rentals from their expenses. Truth is, working from home does cut down on a large portion of the expenses. But what goes unnoticed is that it also slows down your growth. When you have a huge sum to pay as rent every month, you will have to work harder in order to meet those expenses. When your home gives you the privilege to be comfortable and not worry about the monthly rent, your financial goal is different from the person who has to pay rent every month. This may hamper your motivation to work harder and grow. It's very important to step out of your comfort zone. Only then will you be able to grow and taste success.

Any business takes baby steps growth-wise in the initial years, but when it does flourish, the growth is exponential. This is when owning an office space acts as a hindrance towards growth. You cannot expand and change spaces overnight. You will need to consider a thousand different elements before buying a new property for expansion, the most important here being the finances. But if your office space is rented, you can easily switch to other rented property whenever there is a need for expansion. I have seen a lot of people stable and comfortable in their self-owned business/office property and not grow because of the same reason.

Funds play a major role in this decision. When you plan to expand your business, it requires a lot of funds. And investing in the business and property at the same time is not a feasible option. People shy away from moving into a rented space from a self-owned property. And this is when owning a property comes in the way of expansion of your business.

Similar facts apply when your business hits a block and you need to contract your business. With rented property, you can easily shift to a smaller area and a different location without any restrictions.

In both cases, when you do not have the flexibility in terms of working space, your vision gets blocked and that makes it difficult to think of expansion or contraction as and when the markets demand.

A rented property, on the other hand, gives you the motivation to work harder and put in all your efforts towards achieving your goals. It gives you the flexibility to grow with time and expand your team with changing circumstances.

"They can buy an estate when they want to invest but they should invest in the business when they want to expand."

4.2 GROWTH, ALL ALONG

"When you stop growing you start dying."

– William S. Burroughs

It is an unsaid fact that you are either moving forward or simply losing it. There is no middle ground. You need to be in a constant state of learning and growing to reach the pinnacle of success. This is what makes you more valuable.

The secret to any successful business is to sell more and this is no rocket science. But, how to sell more is important. There are three major ways to increase your sales and focusing equally on all three will end up increasing it by manifold.

- Add more customers
- Sell more to your customers
- Sell more frequently to your customers

In terms of business too, growth is crucial for long-term survival. A business is considered growing when it expands in more ways than one. As a financial advisor, you need to grow constantly in all the aspects to multiply your business manifold. Sales, clients, products and geographical boundaries are the various aspects which need your parallel attention so as to multiply business year after year. Selling more is the key to the growth of any business. The only way to increase revenue is to sell more and more to an increased number of clients.

Most of the financial advisors focus on adding more clients every year to their basket to increase their sales. I will explain this to you through an example. Assume that you have 100 clients and you are able to add 10 more to your basket this year. You will have 110 clients to sell to in the next year. This is exactly what most consultants do. But, is this enough for your business to multiply? No. This will only add on to your sales and will lead to a gradual growth process.

I do not believe in only adding to my business. I work hard every single day to multiply my business. I will tell you how. I also add new products to my business every year. In fact, it is easier to add products and increase your revenue than adding new clients every year. Suppose you choose to sell a Product B in addition to Product A (the one that you were already selling). And if you are able to convince 60 of your clients to buy Product B, then your total revenue will be 110A+60B in the following year. If you are not willing to add this new product, your revenue will remain at 110A. It is a smart decision to keep adding products to your product category every year or as and when required if you want to grow and expand your business. When you have built trust with your client, it is easier to sell him more products. When he believes in one of your products, he is most likely to believe in other products offered by you too.

This is not enough either. Next is to expand your geographical boundaries. Venture into nearby towns and cities which can be added to your client basket. If you are based out of City X and you add another city, say City Y, then you can sell the same product basket to the new city as well. Focusing on adding geographies will help you multiply your revenue. In case you get 50 new clients in City Y, your total revenue will be (110A+60B) from City X + (25A+25B) from City Y, assuming at least 50% of the clients buy either of the two products.

If you don't plan your business growth considering all the four dimensions, you will have to be satisfied with 150A as revenue by the end of 5 years. But, if you work towards expanding in all directions, imagine the growth that your business will witness after 5 years. It will soar to new heights every year, taking you to the pinnacle of success.

When you expand in all the directions is when you actually start growing. Channel your energies and efforts towards all the aspects of your business and not just on clients. Adding more clients every year, along with increasing the product basket and moving out of your geographical boundary, will help you grow your business exponentially. And this will be termed as growth in its true sense.

"I do not believe in adding to my business, instead, I focus on multiplying it."

4.3 KING TO PAWN

"Everyone is a customer of everyone else."

– Babette Ten Haken

"Everyone is not your customer," – this is said and believed by a lot of business preachers. They believe every business and every product has its own customer base. Fortunately, this principle does not apply to our business. For us financial advisors, from the one who delivers milk to the one who accepts it, all of them are our potential customers. From the king to the pawn, we can be of service to anyone.

The product category may vary from one individual to another, and yet, each and every person that you come across is your prospective client. And if you want everyone to be your customer, you need to add different categories to your product segment and pitch accordingly.

As a social being, we meet new people every other day. Being a financial advisor, this excites me all the time. This is what helps to add clients to my basket. I look out for clients everywhere. Be it my child's school event or while dining out at a restaurant, I keep the businessman inside me working and making mental notes of the people I meet. Then, I scrutinise these people and start to work on the ones that give me good business vibes.

Your job is to be a keen observer who looks out for prospects in each and every person you come across. Once you start eyeing everyone, your brain will take the lead and start functioning in order to turn this prospect into a client. Whenever you are out there for any social gatherings or trade fairs etc., you need to be alert and keep your eyes and ears open throughout.

Whenever I see any such opportunity, I make sure to delegate the lead to my team immediately, also while introducing the prospect to one of my team members to take things forward. This leads to multiplied business year after year. Right from my family doctor to my friend's lawyer, I have seen prospects in each of them and turned at least 80% of them into my clients.

From friends to family to your vendors and employees too, everyone can be your target client. If I talk about myself, all my employees and vendors are my clients. Even my driver runs a Systematic Investment Plan (SIP) under my company.

Basically, the products that you and I deal in as financial consultants are required by one and all at different stages of their life. You can help everyone get financial knowledge and boost up their savings. You can serve every person that you meet. What you need to do is keep collecting the data, scrutinise them, prioritise accordingly and start following up.

"Once you start eyeing everyone, your brain will take the lead and start functioning in order to turn this prospect into a client."

4.4 NEW BONDS OVER OLD

"You don't build a business, you build people and then those people build business."

– Zig Ziglar

Business relationships are those assets which do not appear on the balance sheet but are definitely the most valuable of all resources. They require a strong foundation of amicability and trust. And it is very difficult to change a satisfied customer's mind. Most of the prospective clients that I approach tend to put forward already established relationships as the reason for not giving me business. They have business relationships dating to decades back, which they are not ready to forgo or any new advisor. They are so happy with their existing advisor that they don't see any reason to break ties with th. Some are even aware that they can earn higher retu if their money is invested elsewhere. But the old bonc ps them from trying out new advisors. These ties act as tleneck in acquiring new clients.

I tr cus on the solution more than the problem. And th ow I came up with a plan to face this challenge sed that there is this strong emotional connectio stops a person from forming new business relationships. So, there is only one way of breaking this chain. It's a newer, stronger bond, over and above the former one. Only when you build a much stronger bond with your prospect than the bond which he has with his current advisor will you then be able to get his business.

Generally, when I go to a prospective client, he mentions his hesitation to say no to his existing service provider for the sole reason of being in business terms with him since ages. You need to work on building a stronger bond with him which makes him refrain from saying no to you in future. Get so close and familiar with your client that he decides to say no to his current advisor and not you.

This is your chance when he starts by giving you partial business if not completely. Now is the time for you to prove your capabilities. Once you have entered a new family, earned a new client and got some of his business, it is totally up to you to convert this partial business in 100% of the client's portfolio.

Another way to board a client on the basi f a relationship is to become their customer first. pose one of the prospects that you have been eye eals in something that you have been looking to bu ome his customer. A small analogy will help you stand this better. Last year, I had to buy a cell r my wife. Previously, I used to buy cell phon a shop in my area. But this time, I chose to b another store which had multiple outlets. I knew it would be a little more expensive to buy the cell phone from that store, yet I didn't hesitate even once. The sole reason behind it was to establish a bond with the owner of that store. I had been looking out for him for a long time and this was a perfect opportunity. After that, I made multiple purchases from him over a year as and when needed. This helped me establish a great relationship with him and I was able to convert him into my customer.

All this might take some time and a lot of effort from your end, but you will get business only when you manage to break old ties and form new relationships. Stronger, newer bonds are the only way out for old business relationships.

Don't give up; instead, keep following up with a positive mindset and believe that you will crack the deal some day: could be next month, next year or even after a decade. But, do not shy away from trying and working hard till you succeed.

"I realised that there is this strong emotional connection which stops a person from forming new business relationships."

4.5 BIG INVESTMENTS = BIGGER RETURNS

"You gotta spend money to make money."

– Titus Maccius Plautus

However cliché it may sound, this saying is absolutely true. You need to spend money to make money. The more you invest in your business, the bigger your business gets and hence, the returns rise higher. Your revenue is always in proportion to the investment you make. And this holds true for all kinds of business. Do not back out or act stingy when it comes to investing in your business as it can hamper your growth to a great extent. Invest generously as per requirements and see your business grow and flourish.

In the financial advising business, a lot of them out there believe that you don't necessarily need to invest funds. Many advisors do not invest for years together and still grow. But what they don't realise is that the growth is at a very gradual pace. To experience extraordinary growth, even a financial advisor needs to keep investing in his business.

I would like you to answer a simple question. What do you do with the revenues that you earn from this business of yours? Most people invest their surplus (after keeping a portion for livelihood expenses) in fixed deposits, bonds, mutual funds, etc. But why? Why does anybody need to invest in other products to earn revenue and not in their own business? Do not hesitate to invest in your own business, which will assure higher returns as compared to any other investments. If your business brings in more profit, why not invest the surplus in it and reap its benefits.

Each time I have invested in my own business, I have received multifold rewards. Whether I spend the invested money on technology, infrastructure or on adding more products, manpower to my team and also on marketing, it has always been worth it. This has helped me take my business forward smoothly and has helped it grow exponentially. If I invest an amount X in my business, I am sure to pull X+ amount in the same year itself. There is an added advantage of spending money on your business. When you are aware of spending your hard-earned money on your business in terms of product or IT or anything else, you will work even harder making an energetic commitment to reap the returns of this reinvested amount.

So, instead of investing your revenue on equity of some other company, why not spend it on your own. Once you start following this, you will never regret doing this. Your sole regret would be why you didn't invest earlier. Let your money work for you and reap more and more profits.

Another crucial investment that you need to make as a financial advisor is that of your time. You need a lot of patience and perseverance to work progressively towards your goals. It is one of the most underrated virtues of entrepreneurs in today's time. I will explain the importance of being patient through a little story.

Mr X had opened a restaurant in January 2021. It was his first step in the food industry. He had everything in place before he started operations. Great interiors, superb menu selection and a hard-working and dedicated team. But what he lacked was patience. Rightly said, "Patience is the virtue that doesn't belong to all." He didn't understand that every new business needs some time before it starts giving you profits. In a hurry to reap returns, Mr X set up a cart on wheels outside his restaurant and offered the same menu on the cart. This time, the business picked up rapidly but for the cart. And what do you think happened to the restaurant? It collapsed. Nobody would ever pay a higher price for something that is easily available at a lower price. Mr X had degraded his value out of impatience and this led to the downfall of his restaurant. People always tend to respect those who strive consistently, regardle f the time required to accomplish their goals.

ceed.

You need to be patient and committed money It takes a lot of investment in terms oth time and time to reap the fruits of your b r business and money work hand in hand not function a success. A financial advising ow, you need smoothly by dedicating tim to invest funds smartly from time to time. The key is to practice patience and hard work while keeping the focus on and never giving up.

"Why does anybody need to invest in other products to earn revenue and not in their own business?"

4.6 UP THE DATA GAME

"Regular data inflow leads to regular business deals."

– Unknown

Closing a deal doesn't happen in a single day. The conversion process from a prospective to a customer takes time for all businesses, though the conversion time may vary from one business to another. In the financial services industry, this time also varies from client to client. Some may take a couple of months to get on board while others may make you slog a couple of years before they give you business.

To convert deals regularly, you need to also have leads regularly. You need to work on creating new prospects every single day. I will explain to you why. Suppose you have a list of 100 potential clients and you start working on the same. Let us say, the conversion period is 1.5 years on an average for our business. You manage to close 50-60% of the clients in these 1.5 years, assuming the other lot might take some more time to convert. What will happen after 1.5 years? What will you do if you do not have a new set of 100 clients to focus upon? From where do you plan to grow your revenue if you exhaust your database? Hence, to convert new clients every day, you need to fill in the database pipeline regularly for regular outflow of business. Data integrity is the key and is now more important than ever. It should be at the top of your mind game. Keep doing your homework to constantly add data to your system. This is what will ultimately earn revenue for your business.

This database needs to be really huge. I have enough data to survive me for the next five years at least and I am adding up to it every single day. This has been created so that I and my team do not sit idle for even a day and keep working on it to generate leads and convert them into business. There are certain clients in our database who are to be targeted three years later. We keep exercising on this data for optimum results.

Another important aspect to focus upon is closing business every month. You cannot afford to miss out on any opportunity to generate revenue. Make sure to have a pipeline of closed businesses every month. I have already discussed the importance of adding to the list of prospects every month. Now, I will tell you the need to close business every month and how to go about it.

Collect as much insurance renewal data as possible. The bigger the data the higher the possibility for closed business on a regular basis. As mentioned earlier, don't forget to put reminders for every future opportunity. I have a dedicated team to collect data from clients and update it on my database.

If you are able to collect data of 1000 insurance policies in a year and close nearly 60% of it, then you get 600 policies that year. By the end of the following year, you have data close to 2000 policies. If you are able to renew 90% (600*90% = 540) of your previous year's business and 60% (1400*60% = 840) of the remaining opportunities, then you have 540+840 = 1380 closed businesses. Hence, you will have multiplied business every single day.

Most of the financial advisors have a heavy workload in the last financial quarter. They have a huge number of business deals that close at the end of the financial year. But, my advice is to segregate this workload throughout the year. This way, your pipeline will not get choked at the year end and will function smoothly throughout the year.

Suppose you have 100 business opportunities lined up for the last financial quarter. Try to divide at least half of it throughout the rest of the year, leaving you with half the workload for the last quarter. This will e able easing of your business process and you will have siness throughout the year. Leaving everything f he year end might also lead to lost or reduced bu s because of unforeseen circumstances. Avoiding ast minute hustle is beneficial for both you and y ent.

ome time now

I have been following this for business. A good and it has proved to be effectiv well in advance my database helps me evaluate a I know beforehand schedule for the followin ities that I have to of the possibilities ar look forward to. I know what to focus on and target it accordingly, leading to more conversions.

Working on the data should be your top priority and part of your regular business operations. You need to keep upgrading your data with new clients and also new data of existing clients. You should personally cater to data-building and integrity because without data there is no business at all. Every new data is a new opportunity for you to grab. And collecting data is not enough. That is just the beginning. Working on it and converting it is the real job. Hence, pay complete attention to it before everything else. Only this will lead to regular business and revenue, ensuring long-term growth for your company.

"I have enough data to survive me for the next five years at least and I am adding up to it every single day."

4.7 NO RISK, NO GAIN

"If you are not a risk taker, you should get the hell out of business."

– Ray Kroc

A conservative approach towards business is not something that will take you miles. It is sure to bring you security but not success. Just like the 1s and 2s in a cricket match will keep you in the game but won't end up winning the game for your team. You need to be an aggressive player in your business game too. Move out of your comfort zone and hit hard.

Safe players are not appreciated by most people. They are sure to be shown the door after a couple of matches. But an aggressive player is not held back even if the team has lost a game. This is so because the team knows that his do or die approach will motivate them and help them win eventually.

I am somebody who works not to survive but to succeed and hence, I am always aggressive in my outlook towards my business.

Playing it safe might seem the easiest option for you. But, what you forbid to see are the dangers that tag along while playing it all safe. It is not something that will pop up everyday and unwind in a dramatic fashion. You will never be able to point it out as it is gradual in its process but is lethal at the same time. Clearly the silent killers of any business empire, playing it safe can prove to be quite dangerous.

The biggest risk that any of the financial advisors fear to take is expansion. A lot of money gets involved when you plan to expand either infrastructure-wise or technologically. Also, adding new products is a mental challenge for few advisors. Hence, many of us choose to play safe and settle for what they have, ignoring the danger that lies in not growing with changing times.

Taking risks is a trait every entrepreneur should practice. This does not mean that you go into it blindly without weighing the consequences, careful planning and dedication coupled with hard-work, which are what bring in success. Be aggressive towards all the elements of your business. Be it selling a product, marketing, infrastructure development or retention, you need to be quick enough to make your decisions. You should always be on your toes, ready to plan out and implement it without any delay. If there is a query, you need to be aggressive in replying back and then converting it into a lead and further on turning it into a closed deal. If a client is on the lookout for a product, it needs to be addressed immediately. If you are not active enough, your competitor might get lucky.

You need to keep asking certain questions to yourself first and then also to your team. You should have answers to:

- Where do you see your business in five years?
- What do your clients need today?
- Are you fulfilling them?
- Is your communication effective enough?
- Are you under-utilising your resources?
- How are your competitors better than you?

You need to keep asking these questions incessantly and make your team uncomfortable in search of the answers. This is when you and your team will learn not to settle for less. Not to be lazy and not to be content.

It is natural to gravitate towards playing it safe. But, you as the leader of your team and your life should make it more uncomfortable to play it safe than to keep working towards taking new risks every day. Playing it safe will definitely keep you in the game but what will help you win it is the aggression that you show towards your business and the risks that you are willing to take.

Initially, you might fall, but in the end you will definitely succeed by taking a new risk every time. Don't rush into it, instead, take baby steps but with aggression and see your business reach heights. A lot of you don't take risks with the fear of falling. So the probability of growth becomes zero. But if you try, there is only a probability that you will fail but a chance to grow too.

"Clearly the silent killers of any business empire, playing it safe can prove to be quite dangerous."

5. CUSTOMER IS GOD

"Your smile is your logo, your personality is your business card, how you leave others feeling after an experience with you becomes your trademark."

– Jay Danzie

5.1 STOP THE LEAKAGE

"Your best customers leave quite an impression.
Do the same and they won't leave at all."

– Unknown

No business can afford to dissatisfy its customers. Even offering them a good enough experience and service is going to disappoint them. You have to be at your best all the time. Keeping your commitment to "Client First" should come naturally to you. If you succeed in putting your clients first, you will find that everything else will fall into place–growth, financial security and great goodwill.

There is no business in the world where customers don't drop. As you add new customers to your business every year, there is a percentage of clients who leave. This is a fact which cannot be changed by any means. Leakage of clients is inevitable in any business. But the real problem arises when the rate of drop is higher or even equal to the rate of added customers. For every customer that drops, you need to look back and know where exactly you and your team went wrong. You need to be well aware of the what, where, why and how it went wrong. Only then will you be able to learn from your mistakes and not repeat them in future. The lost customers are sure to lead to decreased revenues. The dent that they create in your pocket might not even be covered up by double the new clients. You cannot guarantee the business any new client is about to give you. But the lost client definitely takes a portion of your business.

Your focus should primarily lie on the retention of your customers. You need to work towards your lost customers too. It is way easier to retain an old customer than to add a new one. On-boarding a new client is always tricky and challenging. So, it is best to retain our existing clients. While adding new customers, many advisors lose focus on the existing ones. Don't forget that these are the ones who give you your daily bread and butter. You cannot afford to lose them.

There are various reasons behind our loyal customers leaving us. According to a survey, 1% of our clients die, 3% migrate to a different city and 5% generate bonds with new financial advisors. About 9% leave because of competition, 14% are dissatisfied with your product or service. The remaining 68% drop because of you or your team's indifferent attitude. It could be because of a misunderstanding between you and your client or some communication gap. It could also be because of false expectations and wrong commitments from your end. All this arises because we start taking our existing clients for granted. We develop a carefree and laid-back attitude towards them, which leads to our downfall. This is what makes them turn their backs to us.

This section of the book emphasises how to keep your customers happy. Your customers should take pride in working with you and boast about the same. He should feel secure in trusting you with his funds and finances. And the following chapters will tell you how you can make this happen.

"If you succeed in putting your clients first, you will find everything else will fall into place–growth, financial security and great goodwill."

5.2 WHO LIKES TO WAIT?

"Good service is good business."

– Siebel Ad

In today's world, consumers shed out their money for convenience and speed. They expect more and more from the businesses they patronise. This results in ever increasing demands from a less patient and lesser tolerant client base. If you fail to respond to the queries and needs of your customers immediately, they will be unhappy and shift to the next big thing. The ego of a client is big and it should not be hurt under any circumstances. If you delay your response or do not satisfy your client's ego, you might as well lose him. Not only this, they will make sure the world knows it too through their social media rants.

So, in order to thrive and grow, only your products are not going to be enough. You need to provide customer service that is convenient and provides instant gratification. The first step towards this is answering your client's call ASAP. After all, who likes to wait? Clients today do not have patience at all. They want their queries to be answered at rocket speed. Their emails, messages, etc. should be taken care of and responded to even before they expect you to. Your team should also be trained to do the same. One negligence from your end and be ready to lose your customer forever.

There are many companies that have stopped waiting in queues for their clients. Instead, the call-back option has come into existence now. In this, the client gives a missed call on the assigned number and the company gets back to the client. This is done so that clients do not have to experience a long wait on calls. People get impatient when they have to wait in long queues on calls or if they have to call multiple times. Hence, make sure to pick up your customer's call instantly. This will make him feel valued and important.

> Hi,
>
> I am a little tied up. Would it be fine if I have someone from my office call you?
>
> For any assistance, contact +919800000000
>
> Regards,
> Garvit Chaharia

At times, it might so happen that you are not in a position to take the call. In such a case, do not make the mistake of rejecting the call. Instead, send a message informing your client that you would call him back ASAP. Also, make sure to mention that one of your team members will connect with him at the earliest. On the other hand, do not forget to delegate the call to your team member ASAP.

Even in the case of emails and messages, you do not have a reply ready all the time. Make sure to send an acknowledgement mail and message. This assures the client that his query would soon be resolved. The following example will help you to understand the importance of instant communication.

When you order a product online and you do not receive an acknowledgement for the order confirmation. Also, if there is no system to track the order, you will be restless till you receive it. You will be in a confused state as to whether your order has been confirmed and dispatched by the team or not. That the product will reach you on time or not will also remain a matter of concern. This will leave you in a stressful situation.

On the other hand, if the company immediately gives you an acknowledgement with the estimated date of arrival of the product, you are at ease. It is an added advantage if the e-commerce company also enables you to track the live location of the product once it is dispatched. Tracking does not reduce the estimated delivery period but it helps you know the whereabouts of the product. And this piece of information satisfies you as a customer and you know that your order is being done. There is always an update for you regarding your product. This instant and regular communication from the company's end makes you feel at ease.

Likewise, any communication from the client's end should not be ignored, rejected or delayed under any circumstances. Solving pain points early on is the quickest way to reduce the stress of a client. Even if the work assigned to you is going to take some time, keeping your client in the loop is important. Do update him that his work is being done. Clients are your priority and your actions should make them feel the same.

> Dear **Rohit** Sir,
>
> **Greetings**!!!
>
> Coming up with a good quote for your proposal might take a couple of days.
>
> We will get back at the soonest.
>
> Thank you for your patience and support.
>
> Regards,
> **Mohit Kumar**

"The ego of a client is big and it should not be hurt under any circumstances."

5.3 LOYALTY IS PRICELESS

"When the customer comes first, the customer will last."

– Robert Half

Customer loyalty is the measure of your client's desire to do repeat business with you. This loyalty comes in only when you are first loyal towards your client. It happens when you choose the client's benefit over and above a particular product or company that you deal in.

Many primitive advisors stick to the product and company that they have been dealing with for years. I know a lot of insurance advisors who have stuck to the companies and products that they have been working with. Also, many advisors are still into post office schemes and other primitive products. Their loyalty lies with the company and the product and not with their clients. These advisors are never keen on working with other companies. They believe in sticking to the company that gave them a start and helped them build their life. Another classic case is when the younger generations refuse to do what their ancestors did not. But they do not realise that they have built a wrong approach towards their business over the years.

When you are loyal towards a company or a product, your offerings to your clients become biased. And this hampers your growth extensively. When you are loyal towards the company and not your client, it reflects in your attitude and, in turn, your business. You forget that a company is for a lifetime but not the client. If the client feels that your proposal is not in favour of his profits, he will never come back to you. He will shut the door on you forever.

It is wise to be loyal towards your client. They are the ones who put food on your plate and keep you alive in the game. So make your client's needs and requirements your top priority. Everything else should be considered secondary. Trust and loyalty is what ultimately leads to a client's willingness to conduct business with you again. Once a client starts believing in you and trusts you with his finances, he will come back to you year after year.

Your assets are the customers that you have earned over the years. Do not misinterpret the products that you have sold or the companies that you have worked with as your assets. Because, if you did not have the customers, who would you sell your products to? So, keep your consumers happy and hold on to them as your biggest assets. Smart businessmen always sell products which their clients demand. Trying to sell something that you think is the best and is not in demand across your client base is a mere wastage of time. If you keep your consumers satisfied, they will forever be loyal to you.

"Your assets are the customers that you have earned over the years."

5.4 ANYTHING FOR HNIS

"Just having satisfied customers isn't good enough anymore. If you really want a booming business, you have to create raving fans."

– Ken Blanchard

We, as financial advisors, must nurture each client as a gardener does each flower in his garden. It is easier for the bigger clients to grab our immediate attention but the smaller ones should not be ignored either. They too may grow into bigger clients with time.

While doing this, your focus should also be on the revenue. You cannot afford to end up wasting time in doing something that does not yield revenue for your company. Your client, irrespective of his stature, will expect you to attend to him and do several operational tasks involving a lot of your time, energy and resources. And, in turn, these operational tasks do not end up giving even a penny for all the hard work put in. This category of work falls into the urgent work slot, irrespective of it not being very important. The sole reason that your client has asked you to do this makes it urgent.

You need to identify the client as big or small when you are asked to perform something that is quite small as compared to the usual business that you do. As an entrepreneur, you are supposed to do all the work for your big clients as well as prospective big clients. You should not leave any opportunity to make them happy. Also, big business from a small client shouldn't be ignored considering his stature. If an HNI client gives you small business, you should consider doing his operational work too as he might give you a huge business later on.

Suppose you are asked to insure a bike for an HNI client or his staff. Irrespective of the revenue you receive from it, I would suggest you consider doing it. But if this is requested from a small client with no potential to grow, try to avoid it by refusing in a polite manner. The idea behind this is to always keep an HNI client happy so that he keeps giving you business in volumes and not wasting your time on small jobs of non-potential clients as it will only suck up your precious time and give you nothing in return. Train your team to take good care of your HNI's team. Guide them to create a web around your client and his team so as to always keep them happy and in turn dependent on you and your team.

There are certain other factors that go behind the work that you do for your clients. Whether a client invests Rs 1000 or Rs 10 lakhs, it is equally important for each of them. So they expect your equal attention and time. Smaller clients are more difficult to handle as they have more concerns and fears, leading to many more queries. Smaller clients are easy to board but very difficult to manage. And HNI clients are challenging to on-board but easier to handle. Now, you need to decide where you want to utilise your time to earn maximum revenue.

I advise you to form a separate team altogether to deal with small business and smaller clients. If a small customer doesn't have a scope to give you a sizeable amount of business, you need to delegate his work to your team. You cannot afford to invest your time, energy and effort in such transactions. When you delegate this kind of work, it doesn't offend your client nor does it suck up your precious time. Hence, leaving a win-win situation for both you and your customers. This delegation of work should be done smartly so that you don't come across as arrogant. Your clients, whether big or small, shouldn't feel offended in any way. This delegation process might take some time to work smoothly but once your team is ready, it is so rewarding. You can then focus on more important work and clients.

I took roughly three years to assign my smaller clients to my subordinates and I couldn't be happier and relaxed. Not that the smaller clients are unimportant to me. I definitely do business with them but through my team. This team also takes care of the employees of my HNI clients. It is very important to keep the team members of my client happy as they are the ones who help me grow even more. The dedicated team makes sure to deal with all such clients.

Divide your clients well on the basis of the business they give you. And then work accordingly. Delegation of smaller clients means that you will not have to say a no to them when both your hands are full with bigger clients. This will also mean no compromise on your quality of work. Keeping all your clients happy is your responsibility. And, in turn, they will help you grow, bigger and better.

"You cannot afford to end up wasting time in doing something that does not yield revenue for your company."

5.5 CLOSED BUSINESS. WHAT NEXT?

"Don't celebrate closing a sale, celebrate opening a relationship."

– Patricia Fripp

Every closed deal is a moment to celebrate with your team members. Only you and your team members are aware of the hard work that goes behind cracking every single deal. But what is your next step? What do you and your team members do once the deal has been finalised with the client? The first step should be to thank your valued customer for placing his trust in you and giving you an opportunity to serve him. Let him know how important every business deal is for your company.

Whenever you onboard a new client, he expects more than just your services. He expects something extra. And you are supposed to give him this extra something. I recommend you to send a handwritten letter to thank him for the trust that he has shown in you, along with the usual mail and message. Create a nice on-boarding message for your clients, which emphasises their contribution towards the growth of your company. This will do wonders by making your client feel special and valued. This is very important because, if the client is big and has the potential, he is sure to give you more business in the future too. But this will happen only when he gets this extra treatment from you and your team.

Also, every time an existing client gives you a new business, make sure to thank the client personally via a message. Even the allotted RM should thank his respective client after they have closed business. This will reassure his trust in you.

> Dear **Rohit Kumar** Sir,
>
> **Thank You** for your valued business.
>
> We are obliged by the trust and confidence you showed in us by giving us an opportunity to serve you.
>
> We promise you an amazing experience.
>
> Looking forward to work with you in the future too.
>
> Regards,
> **Mohit Kumar**

We all have at least one such friend in our lives who calls us only in times of crisis or when he is in need of help. We can't ignore this fact and find that person repulsive. We can't help but think that this friend calls us only when he needs our help and not on any other occasion. There is no fondness for any such person. Don't be this friend to your client. It is important for you to set up reminders for the future once a deal is closed. Your client should never feel that you contact him only for business and that once you get it, you forget him. Put up quarterly reminders to call or visit your client regularly. These meetings are done in order to warm up your relationship with the client. The hidden gain is to gather more knowledge regarding your client's financial data. This is what will provide you with multiple business opportunities all the year round.

In case of a closed deal for an insurance policy, update your system on its renewal date so that you can approach the client timely for renewal. Visualise the renewal as a new business opportunity rather than simple renewal of the same. Keep your focus on upgrading the policy and not simply renewing it. If your client has taken 1 Crore Term Insurance, then you need to educate him on upgrading his sum insured to 2 Crores. He might not take this decision at the end of the first year itself but if you keep updating him on the benefits of upgrading every year, most likely he will come around after a few years. Also, you can propose to him to switch to a different insurance company which offers a lower premium or an increased amount of sum insured. This will lead to the client's benefit and also yours in terms of added revenue.

Redemptions do happen in case of investments. What will you do if your client asks to pull out his funds owing to personal needs or other reasons and informs you that he would be happy to continue with investments after six months? The first thing is to call up and check whether your client has received the funds and the statements smoothly. Next, you need to set a reminder for five months after redemption to follow up with your client.

The focus here should be to get the SIP restarted and, if possible, with an increased amount.

It is very crucial for you to get in touch with your client at least three to four times before the actual business is to take place. Keep approaching them again and again, which sets an expectation in their mind all year round. This will convince them that you will offer them a deal when the time comes. Clients cannot be moulded in a day. Prepare them gradually to accept or at least consider the deal offered by you.

This is true also in case of a prospective business opportunity where you are waiting to on-board a client. Turning up with a quotation 15 days before the renewal will not get you business. Set reminders for every three months and meet the client so that you can scale up your relationship with him.

And make the final move 45 days prior to the renewal date. If you approach him two months prior, he might feel it is too early and 15-20 days in advance will be too late for you. You can communicate to the client that it is time for his policy's renewal or redemption and reinvestment. You can inform him that you are working on the quotation and would like to know if there are changes to be made to provide him with the best quotation. The objective is to sense the mood of the client and also give him the quotes at least 30 days before the renewal date. These days, warming up your relationship and providing the quotes to your client should be enough for you to win over your competitor.

Only closing the deal will not help you grow. Following up is crucial when a deal is closed and also when you lose a business. The reminders are very important in both cases to create new business opportunities for you.

"Whenever you on-board a new client, he expects more than just your services."

5.6 LOVE TO EARN

"It's easier to love a brand when the brand loves you back."

– Seth Godin

In business, love is always more than a feeling; it is a person's individual choice. And this love shouldn't just be there in the initial days of the business transaction. It should only grow with time. Learn to love your clients to earn them.

Loving your client is not always easy, especially in the financial industry. You come across people from diverse backgrounds. It may happen that your client is not good looking, doesn't dress up well and his choice of words may be a matter of concern to you. You might not be really fond of his attitude too. Right from impeccably dressed clients to the ones who are in *dhotis* and *lungis*, you got to love them all. The smokers to the tobacco chewers, anybody could be a part of your clientele. You might not be able to stand certain habits of your clients but that's not the real problem. The challenge here is in not making the other person realise what you think and feel about him. You have to mould yourself to like and respect them. Even if for an instance you make them feel uncomfortable or disliked, they might not turn to you for advice. You need to develop a liking for your clients and this will bring them back to you.

I will explain this to you through a very simple example. Suppose you go to buy a cigarette at a shop. And his owner throws the box of cigarettes towards you and asks you to help yourself as he is preoccupied. On the other hand, there is another shopkeeper in the same locality who welcomes you with a big smile. Assume that he also offers to light your cigarette and strikes a conversation with you every time you visit him. Which shop would you prefer to go to? Undoubtedly, the latter, right? The reason behind is the attitude of the shopkeeper and not the product. You need to understand that your attitude towards your client is very important when it comes to client satisfaction and retention.

Expecting your client to change is foolish. He will not alter because you don't like him. And you cannot afford to lose a client for a silly reason like this. If you fail to develop a liking towards him, how do you expect him to like you and choose you as his service provider over others? How do you plan to do justice to your profession? Will you be able to hide this dislike? Will you be able to give 100% to that client? Of course, not. Love your client and make sure it comes across to him and ends up making him feel special and important.

"Learn to love your clients to earn them."

5.7 WOW, I WON!

"Obligatory business is the end, not the beginning."

– Unknown

Most of us keep our to-do lists ready to refer and follow. We always focus on what to do to grow in our business. But, there are times when you also have to decide on what not to do to grow. Never underestimate the power of what not to do in certain circumstances. The foremost is not to do obligatory business ever.

Many times, your deal might not close because of certain factors. Some people may not be excited about your product while in other cases, the timing might be incorrect. But in any case, you need to keep following up with your clients and keep marketing your brand to them. Clients or not, you should not miss out on making them a part of your team. But this should never end up in a business deal which the client offers to you out of obligation. A client shouldn't offer a business to you just because you have been following up with him for a long time. And if he does so, I would not advise you to accept the offer. Also, some clients offer business to you only because you have been referred to by somebody. Obligatory business purely out of reference shouldn't be accepted either.

You might feel that it would be the start for you. But I think otherwise. I feel it is like shutting the door on you after offering you peanuts. I think a client offers a small business as he cannot or does not want to offer you anything big and can't say no to you either. It is like offering a lollipop to a child who has been after your life for a toy. This lollipop is to shut his mouth forever.

Never focus on this type of business. You might be of the opinion that being at the receiver's end you are not entitled to say no. You must also be wondering that a business is a business irrespective of its size. The client might get even more difficult to on-board once you refuse the peanuts offered by him. Even if it is the first step towards your client, I would suggest against it. Whenever a client offers a business which reeks of obligation, say no to it. And say it in a dignified way which doesn't offend your client. Tell him that you will wait for a good business deal with him when he has full confidence and faith in you. Let him know that you would be happy to serve him when he is willing to work with you and not when he feels obliged to do so. If you accept such business, all your prior efforts will go down the drain.

I can tell you from my experience that obligatory business is never long-term. It is just a subtle way of showing you the door. In my earlier days, it has happened with me on a number of occasions. Once, a client offered me 5 lakhs to invest in mutual funds. And later, he redeemed it without my knowledge. After that, I didn't have the face to go to him again. The doors were shut from all sides. I realised that I had made him take this route of saying no and made it easier for him.

So, the idea is to change their perception about you. Tell them way in advance that you are not there to get obligatory business. It is totally up to you to be happy with small deals or have patience and grab a bigger one. Your attitude should be such that your client doesn't offer you obligatory business. He should be well aware that you will not accept it. I have one such client whom I have been following up with for the past seven years. But he has offered me obligatory business on a couple of occasions. But, I chose not to accept them. I kept following up with him while maintaining a healthy relationship throughout. So, I considered his doors open for me. Finally, I was able to close a big deal with him recently when he developed full faith in me and looked forward to working with me.

I will explain to you why it is important for the client to be willing to work with you. When I had started college, I expressed my desire to own a bike to my dad. Like most fathers, he was reluctant at first but eventually came around. He agreed that I needed a vehicle and zeroed upon a scooter instead of a bike. He explained to me how his friend had suggested taking a scooter and not a bike, keeping my safety in mind. I had no other choice but to agree. I was happy that I had a vehicle to myself but there was always an itch that I didn't get something that I had willingly chosen. A few months down the line, I started looking for options and ways to replace the scooter with a bike. And I kept doing this until I actually found an exit plan and bought a bike.

Likewise, if your client chooses you only because you have been referred to by someone or because you have been constantly following up, he is sure to replace you even before you realise. He will keep looking for exit options and find an advisor of his choice.

Your client can consider you if someone referred you, but he should choose you only out of his willingness to work with you. Only then will your relationship grow and last long. The amount of business is not as important as his inclination towards you. Once he chooses to give you business, he will continue to do so without any hesitation or mental block. This relationship based on his choice and faith in you is sure to go a long way.

"Obligatory business is never long-term. It is just a subtle way of showing you the door."

5.8 THE LIFELINE: COMMUNICATION

"When it comes to business you don't need to learn a new language, you just need to manage a communication tool."

– Kenneth OE Sundin

Global business is mostly dependent on communication. Be it any industry, space, technology or entertainment, nothing works without communication. Millions of pounds are being spent on transmitting data and making communication effective in each field.

Communication is vital for every relationship to grow and last forever. In all facets of business too, communication plays a fundamental role. Open channels of communication help in leading to new ideas and innovations. Hence, it is very important that both internal and external communications are effective for the smooth functioning of a company. Faster, safer and clearer communication is what will make you stand out from your competitors. Communication with the clients, communication with your team members and communication with the vendors are the pillars of the financial services industry.

Great communication in advisor-client relationships is an important aspect of our business to establish early on. It can increase your client's trust in you, increase your popularity with clients and help wonders in tricky situations as communication makes it easier to resolve issues.

Your client is always on the lookout for an honest, accurate and transparent company to work with. It is, therefore, very important to include this in the very nature of your work ethic. You need to understand the importance of explaining the products, sharing information and regular updates with the client. This will make the client more understanding and patient.

Congratulations! Your health insurance policy has arrived.

Mohit | Deeva Ventures Pvt Ltd
rohit@xyz.com

Health Insurance.pdf

Dear **Rohit Kumar**,

Greetings!!!

We believe that your experience of buying insurance with us has been enjoyable. It is a pleasure for us to be able to provide you with your health insurance policy.

Please find attached your health insurance policy.

We wish to make your overall experience wholesome and more convenient by offering you a bunch of other financial products as well under one roof.

We are excited to help you.

Thanks & Regards,

Deeva Ventures Pvt Ltd.
D - 123, XYZ Tower
ABC Road, Varanasi - 221001
Ph: +919800000000
Email: info@deevaventures.com
Website: www.deevaventures.com

INVESTMENT | LOAN | INSURANCE

SINCE 2008

Varanasi's No.1 Financial Market Place

Being in regular contact with your client will increase their trust in you. Throughout the year, you get multiple opportunities to communicate with your client. Utilise these opportunities to the best of your ability. Remain as easily accessible to your clients as possible. This will instil confidence in the client, making him aware that he is important to you.

Monthly emails can be sent to the clients informing them about new products. Quarterly statements are also effective tools of communication. But how will you make sure that these emails are read? Only sending them from time to time without them being read is a waste of your effort. A communication is complete and considered successful only when both the sender and receiver are clear in correspondence. The sender ID should have your name and also your company's name in it so that the receiver knows that the email was sent by you.

Draft your emails well so that it is a delight for the customers. Crisp language, along with an attractive subject line, is the highlight of a well-drafted email. The objective should not be to simply write the email, instead, to write it really well. Your main content should be added in the email body itself and not as an attachment as most of the attachments go ignored.

Have a goal-based approach towards communication. The purpose of the communication should be to reach the client and not just for us to send it. For instance, a client has requested a particular statement to be sent to him. Somebody from your team does the needful. Do you think your job is complete here? If yes, then you are highly mistaken. What will happen in case your client is not regular on emails or your email lands up in the spam box or gets lost amongst the hundreds of emails that he receives? He will miss out on the email sent by your team and assume that you have ignored his request. Instead, send the statement through WhatsApp, email and a hard copy too, if required. Also, inform the client that the needful has been done through a personal message or call by your team. Communicate in multiple ways so that the information to be shared reaches the client through every means. This ensures that he will definitely receive it through at least one of the mediums.

Communication within your team is also very important for the smooth functioning of all the various business operations. Every piece of data that you receive from the client should be sent to your team at rocket speed so as to not miss out on any opportunity. This shared data will in turn help you and your team to close business. I have made it a point to share data with my team as and when I receive it. Irrespective of the time, I ensure to communicate the relevant information to the dedicated RM immediately via message or email so as to not let go of any business. Do not postpone it under any circumstances or else you might forget about it totally. Prioritise this communication and you will notice how effective it is in your day to day functioning.

Keep communicating with the company whose products you deal in. This helps you grow as an advisor as you keep updating yourself on the knowledge of new products and market conditions.

Communication on all the three aspects of the financial services world is crucial. Especially the one with the clients is incredibly important in today's times. Lagging behind on even one of the aspects could be hazardous for your company.

Our service industry is entirely based on relationships. Communication is the key when it comes to building strong relationships and it should not be overlooked. Effective communication can be a challenge but if done skilfully, it can lead you to success.

"Open channels of communication help in leading to new ideas and innovations."

5.9 MAKE IT EASY

"There is a place in the world for any business that takes care of its customers–after the sale."

– Harvey MacKay

When clients start working with new advisors, first impressions mean everything. Getting a client on board is one of the initial interactions between the advisor and the newly won client. The advisor's communicative approach affects the client-advisor relationship from the beginning and has lasting effects moving forward.

Easing out the workings of a financial deal is a big relief that you can give to your customers. Start with having easy conversations with them so that they understand everything thoroughly. Right from the product to its benefits and limitations, everything should be well-explained to the clients. Next step involves the documentation work. Once the deal is finalised, you should get ready with the list of documents that you would need from the clients. There is no harm in asking for extra documents that you might need in future. But do not make the mistake of asking for documents again and again. This will irritate your client and leave a bad impression in the start itself. He might misunderstand you for an inept advisor and doubt your knowledge.

The forms should be double-checked before sending them to your clients for signatures. Usually, advisors put a tick mark on places where the client is required to sign. But I do not support that. In fact, my team makes a big circle in pencil wherever the client has to sign. This can be erased later. Also, they count the number of signatures to be done in a particular form and write the number at the top of the form. This enables the client to count his signatures and confirm in turn, leaving no room for error. My team also makes a list of documents to be attached and make a note of the same for the client's knowledge.

At the time of closing the deal, it is important for you to ask your client for an alternate person from his team to converse with. Having one point of contact is very important as it smoothens the process of data collection, other relevant information and documentation. If not available, only then is it advised to contact the client for everything. If he suggests you a POC, then the client can delegate his work to his subordinates and be at ease. This also applies to you. You can introduce your back office team to the client's POC. The client need not be disturbed for every little detail that you might need. And, even you will be free to close other deals while your team takes care of the post-deal workings.

And talking about online transactions, these processes have been smoothened even more. The lengthy documentation process is found repulsive by most of the clients and this is where online transactions come in handy. They reduce the workload to a major extent by eradicating the pain in signing multiple papers. I remember on-boarding an HNI client with 15 different accounts to be opened, which included 6 individual accounts, 4 minor accounts, 2 proprietorship accounts, 2 private ltd. accounts and 1 trust account. You can imagine the documentation involved. I was able to complete all the formalities within three days straight because of the online mode. My client was overwhelmed with the process as it was unbelievably smooth and hassle-free for him. He commended the easy–to-understand emails which my team had sent him to guide through the process. Technical stuff bounces over a layman's head and it's our duty as an advisor to identify this limitation and simplify it for our clients.

Only advising the best products is not enough. The entire process of understanding a product and buying it to ultimately redeem it should be smooth and also safe for the client. The easier you make everything for your clients, the more they will bank upon you.

"The advisor's communicative approach affects the client-advisor relationship from the beginning and has lasting effects moving forward."

6. THE COMPANY REPRESENTATIVES (CR's)

"Be a sponge and absorb as much information as possible from as many people as possible."

6.1 STICK TO PROFESSIONALISM

"You must have a supplier relationship of constant improvement."

– W. Edwards Deming

We deal in a number of financial products in our industry and each product is unique in its own way. To make the perfect sales pitch, you need to have complete knowledge of each of the products that you deal in. This product knowledge and specifications are provided by the company representatives. They are the ones who update us from time to time about the new products, revenue structure, recent strategies and everything else that revolves around the product. In a way, we are dependent to a large extent on the company representatives for the guidance required to be well-versed with products and updates too. This is what helps a financial advisor in recommending the right products to the right client base. A healthy relationship with the company people sets the tone right for the smooth functioning of the business. The relationship managers help you negotiate a better percentage of revenues from the company and also help you bag better deals.

The relationship that you and the company's representatives have should be clearly defined. Keeping it thoroughly professional is very important. Mixing business and pleasure is never a smart choice. The product knowledge and updates are definitely required but this shouldn't be an excuse to spend a lot of time with the relationship managers of the company. Their job is to spend maximum time with financial advisors like us and visit us as often as possible so that they can influence us to give them more and more business. Allocate a dedicated time slot for the relationship managers and meet them accordingly. You need to understand that the time spent with them is not going to earn revenue for you. You need to draw a line and restrict your meetings with them so as to give maximum of your time to client meetings. Dedicate your valuable time for meetings which will ultimately give you revenue and help you grow.

Suppose you deal in products of 30 companies and the representatives from these companies visit you once a month. Now, if you decide to meet each of them every single time, you will end up losing at least 30 hours a month. These 30 precious hours could easily be used to meet clients and ultimately earn revenue.

A lot of advisors I know go to company offices to get their work done and believe that spending time there will enhance their knowledge about the industry and will help them to get updated. I have consciously decided to not visit any company's offices and engage in conversations which do not help me in earning revenue. Instead, I choose to spend time with my clients who help me grow. In case you require some information on a product or a work done, you can call them anytime and ask them to meet.

If you choose to meet them regularly, then you might end up being biased towards a particular company or product, depending on your relationship with the CR.

I know a lot of financial advisors who take favours from the CRs. But what they fail to realise is the burden they take on themselves by accepting these offers and favours. When you are under the burden of a favour, you end up recommending that particular company's product more than any other product, irrespective of the client's needs. When you accept the deals, you give them the authority to ask you to advise their products and you have to do the same in return.

In spite of being in this industry for more than a decade, I have never fulfilled any company's target. I make sure to not treat the company targets as my own. I have never involved myself in any such commitments, thereby restricting myself from selling wrong products. Barring a couple of occasions in the initial stages of my career, I have stopped going on any group tours sponsored by the company as incentive. The reason being, I do not wish to spend a lot of time with my competitors as the environment around them exerts negative energy.

Another reason to not accept even family vacations is that I do not want to get lured by these offers and engage in mis-selling of any sort. I prefer keeping my portfolio healthy and, in turn, my client's portfolio happy. I am not advising against higher incentives. Definitely negotiate as much as you can to earn maximum revenue, but do not take anything that is over and beyond the ethical revenue.

The CRs often invite advisors for drinks and dinner. Also, many product launches are held along with meet and greet events. These events are held with the sole motive of increasing their sales by influencing us to sell their products over and above other products. The major audience of such events are your competitors who add negativity to the ambience. I strongly recommend you to stay away from such events and gatherings. It is better to stay focused on your business rather than attending such meets.

I have always refrained myself from attending company get-togethers as I believe it is more fruitful to give time to client meetings and business. And, beyond my working hours, I have always preferred family over everything else. If at all I have to attend social events, I choose the one where I find prospective clients and not my competitors.

Do not take any favour from company representatives, be it cash or in kind. This will ensure that you take unbiased decisions on selecting and recommending products to your clients. Stick to your own game plan rather than the one suggested by the company.

Many times, it so happens that you ask the company's RM to get a work done but he doesn't pay heed to it. In such a case, you should be strict enough to get it done. Having friendly relationships with the RMs will prove to be a bottleneck in getting work done. Their job is to help you grow in your business by supporting you as and when needed. Trying to establish a friendship with them will demand your loyalty towards them. As discussed earlier, stick to being loyal to your client first and then towards the company.

The CRs are the ones who help you to run your business without any restrictions. Their constant support and motivating attitude is crucial for your company's survival. Working hand in hand with the CRs is sure to be a win-win for both the parties.

"Mixing business and pleasure is never a smart choice."

7. THE TEAM

"No matter how brilliant a strategy, if you're playing a solo game, you'll always lose out to a team."

– Reid Hoffman

7.1 TRUST THE PROCESS

"Without trust we don't truly collaborate, we merely coordinate or, at best, cooperate. It is trust that transforms a group of people into a team."

– Stephen M.R. Covey

Business is war. Of course, the civilised version of war. Competitors, not countries, are the battlefield rivals. In primitive days, an entire army was trained to go out on the battlefield with the king and help the king win the war. The pawns were neither authorised nor capable enough to defeat or kill the king of the opposing team. Yet, they were the ones who helped their king defeat the opponent and win the battle.

Likewise, you need a team in your business too. You are the one who will win over the client and not your team members. But, you definitely need the team to on-board a client and run the business smoothly. When you have your team in place, you have a system to lean back upon. You can let your team send in quotations and also give presentations on your behalf: all this under your supervision. If an error is committed, you are there to correct them and mend their mistakes. But, if you do not have a dedicated team working for you, there will be no room for correction. There will be nobody to take responsibility for the mistakes. Who will correct you if you are the one making mistakes?

In our industry, advisors are apprehensive when it comes to hiring people. The major reason is the ease of entering our industry. You fear that your employee might turn into an advisor himself and win over your clients. But, what you fail to understand is, this is just a probable situation and not a thing bound to happen. Focus on something that will certainly happen if you hire people, your growth. Your employees will help your business function with ease. Form a skilled, effective and updated team that will assist you in your business and help in its multifold growth.

Only forming a team is not enough though. Trusting and training your team is very important to achieve the desired results. Many advisors hire people but do not give them any authority or share any kind of client data with them. Not giving enough data to the employees will only decrease their efficiency. You need to know that your clients do business with you because you are the face of your company and not your employees. Your clients give business to you because of the trust that you have built over them and because of the huge team that you have. It is your company's branding and goodwill that works in your favour. Make your team recognise this fact and accept it too. No matter how skilled your employee is, he will never be able to match up to you and your stature. And hence, cannot steal your clients.

Your team is your support system. They work on your command. Give them access to data and also the clients. If you do not trust your employees and restrict their working, you will only slow down their efficiency and, in turn, your growth. Instead, prepare a team that understands your worth. Train them well so that they start believing in you. Every team meeting should begin with praising your employees for their hard work and dedication and end with the message that your team is because of you and the company they work for. They should be aware of the fact that all the business your company gets is solely because of you and your network, the company's working and goodwill. The team only helps to grow business and not get business, and this should be brought to their notice from time to time.

Make your team realise that they are in contact with the client because they have your support and backing. Without your name, no client will entertain them ever. The process that they have been taught by you is bringing in business and not them. When the team is told this on repeated counts, they will start believing in you more and more. They will understand that they are valuable only with your support. That is when they will not try to leave your organisation and stick around. When they realise that they cannot get clients on their own, they will not venture out to become advisors.

There are always exceptions to everything and this is not different either. The percentage of employees opting out to work on their own is very high in our industry.

And there is nothing that you can do about it. Instead, bring a change in the way you train your team and focus on the company's growth. Hire people who can help you in this. The following chapters will guide you on how to form an effective team who stays with you.

"Prepare a team that understands your worth."

7.2 OLD IS GOLD

"If you take care of your employees, they will take care of your customers and the business will take care of itself."

– J. W. Marriott

Employee retention is as important as client retention. There is a direct correlation between the two. If you can retain your best employees, you can very well retain your top clients too. Something that takes place inside the organisation reflects on the outside of its customers too.

Retaining talent in the form of employees is of utmost concern in today's market. By focusing on employee retention, you can retain motivated workers who truly want to be part of the company and who believe in the common goal as you, i.e. the company's overall success. It is said that "Old is gold" for a reason. Employees who leave without prior notice can hamper the company's growth in more ways than one. It could be the tipping point and push other valued employees to think about leaving too. It would at least leave a dent in the minds of other team members, which could undermine work performance.

Employee turnover is extremely expensive considering the number of employees who quit their job in search of something better. Some estimates suggest that it can cost an employer double an employee's salary to replace them when they quit. It is different for different industries, and for some it can be even higher.

According to a survey, 45% of employees who quit do so because of salary. Now, if I talk about our industry, most advisors weigh an employee's salary with the sales he brings in. That is when the employer feels that the employee's salary cannot be justified and he is being paid more. This leads to over expectations. On the other hand, the employee feels underpaid. As an advisor, you need to understand that an employee's salary needs to be calculated in terms of the time and effort that he puts in instead of the sales that he brings in.

In our industry, only the owner brings in business and does sales. But he is able to do so only when his team is taking care of other work to smoothen your sales. Financial stability always motivates a person to stay in his job. It is in the nature of a human to work more when he gets more. Pay your employees well and watch them stay put with you for years.

This is important and necessary for most but not enough. In order to retain employees, you must be compassionate towards them. This is a prerequisite over and above everything else. Only paying them well will not make them stay. The right attitude towards them will. No strategy will overcome a lack of empathy for your employees. Give them a proper workplace with extra amenities. Proper cubicles, lunch room, coffee machine and RO water are some of the basic facilities I give to my employees. Unlike other employers, I do not restrict the number of beverages for my team. I make sure they have food on time, irrespective of the workload they have because, at the end of the day, we are all working hard to put food on our plates.

I celebrate the birthdays of each of the team members in my office to make them feel valued and important. I also celebrate after closing big business deals in order to stay connected with my team and boost their morale by making them a part of the celebrations. I do not set any sales targets for my employees but I make sure to incentivise them whenever they help me close a deal.

Praise in public and criticise in private is the thumb rule to be followed under all circumstances. Whenever an employee makes a mistake, try to be solution-oriented instead of emphasising on the problem. Put the problem aside and look for a solution. This will take care of your employee's ego and help in retention to a great extent. And appreciating employees for their good work publicly will always make them do more than you expect out of them.

Each person has their own set of skills and weaknesses. Usually, one tends to focus on the weaknesses of employees and try to improve the shortcomings, which lowers their efficiency and also might lead to hampering their ego. But, my advice is to pay attention to the skills and ignore the weak points. For example: A cricket team's coach would never ask his bowler to work on his batting ability. He would always suggest the bowler to keep practicing bowling and improve his skills. This is done so that the sportsman performs best in his skill. Your employees should also be allowed to perform well in their areas of interest rather than in areas you want them to perform.

Retention also depends to a great extent on the employer, i.e. you. Employees want to add value to themselves and keep growing each day. They want to work in an environment that educates them. An employee should look up to his employer and be in awe of his business sense. He will feel so only when you keep updating yourself from time to time and keep learning more and more. An employee should always feel that he has so much to learn from you. This will always keep him grounded and make him believe that he is dependent on you. He should never feel that he has learned everything from you because if he ever feels so, he will quit. Employee retention will happen only when the employee sees continuous opportunities of growth within the organisation that he works for.

The working process of an organisation matters a lot in employee retention. My company follows a very unique style to get the most out of employees and keep them happy too. We work from 10 am to 7 pm for just 5 days a week. Saturdays are half days focused on training, previous week's reviews, future planning and also to finish the leftover work for the week. All our celebrations are also scheduled on Saturdays as there is no rush to go back to the cubicles to work and also to not hamper the work on weekdays. This results in the team not being overburdened at any point of time. No business on Saturdays is the rule that I follow to run the business smoothly and for long.

Employees work for money, respect, knowledge and growth. If you give them everything they will never leave you.

"It is in the nature of a human to work more when he gets more."

7.3 RISE ABOVE EXPECTATIONS

"Don't blame people for disappointing you, blame yourself for expecting too much from them."

– Unknown

Most of the employers make a huge mistake of having extraordinary expectations from their employees. While hiring, the employers pay high attention to the skill sets and don't clearly lay out the responsibilities or expectations from their employees. As discussed earlier, expectation and goal-setting should always be unambiguous in all cases, including employee hiring.

A lot of advisors anticipate their employees to bring incremental business for them from the very first day. However, this may be demoralising for the employees and may turn out to be counter-productive as they are required to perform and deliver the results on the first day of joining the organisation, without even getting the time to settle in. One needs to rekindle their journey while dealing with the new employees in the initial days of your career path in the industry. Did you deliver on the first day? Did you learn everything that the industry had to offer in the first few days? The answer would most likely be a No. For most people, despite the educational background, on-the-job training and various resources take years to achieve the pinnacle that you are at today, especially in the highly competitive industry like ours. As such, you need to be empathetic towards the employees, motivate them and provide them with the necessary resources and guidance to bring out the best in them, and match their education and skills to optimise organisational goals.

Keeping the employees on a trial basis does not benefit in the long run as there is no ownership by the employees and it is difficult to show any kind of results in this short time. Instead, focus on a person's skills before hiring him. If you really want your employees to show results, train them well. Educate them by sharing your knowledge, guide them at every step and see how they learn to walk on your path. Align employees' goals with that of the company and see how they do wonders for you. Invest your time and update them; only then they will start working like you.

I never set any sales targets for my team but I definitely make sure to incentivise them whenever they earn deals for the company. This also boosts their motivation to perform better and fulfil organisational goals as their own. The operational team also gets rewarded well and, as a result, there is a smooth coordination between the sales and the operational teams.

Great leaders are those who can make more leaders like them. Making a clone of you is the smartest move that you can make in favour of your company. The focus should be on preparing the next-generation leaders who can then even exceed the milestones set by you. Learn to trust your employees and delegate work to them. You should know how to make your employees work for you and towards the organisation's goals. Don't hesitate to share your skills and techniques with your employees in the fear of being betrayed by them. Share your experiences, expertise, proficiencies and the knack to fetch more and more business for you.

Dedicate a fixed time to train them and lay out the procedures, annuals, guidebooks, etc., detailing the flow charts for carrying out even the minutest of tasks. Right from introducing themselves to the client to carrying out the follow-ups after a closed deal, and continuous monitoring on an on-going basis thereafter, you need to impart the best of industry knowledge to your team. However, at the same time, the employees should be given the freedom to ideate and think out of the box to provide superior results. One should be open to opinions and views of the subordinates who can bring a breeze of fresh air essential for the industry. This will help the business grow multifold when everyone in the company is working towards a common goal.

"The focus should be on preparing the next generation leaders who can then even exceed the milestones set by you."

8. LAST BUT NOT THE LEAST

"The best investment you can make is in yourself."

– Warren Buffett

8.1 ATTITUDE MATTERS

"Love your profession. It's a sign of being successful."

– Smurti Paik

A lot of people dislike the job or profession they are in. They always live with the thought that their life would have been better if at all they were into something other than their current job. But trust me, there is nothing called the new dream job. You need to love your current profession to grow in it. Don't be passionate about your profession; be passionate about how well you do in it.

With this outlook, you can succeed in any business. When you learn to love your job and enjoy it too, new opportunities come knocking in. You start to put in all your efforts with reformed energy. Prioritising your business over everything else happens only when you enjoy your work thoroughly. A wanderer is able to explore many different locations only because of his love for travelling. Likewise, you will grow in your business only when you dedicate more time to it and put your 100% effort.

Coming to the financial advising business, a lot of people hesitate to market themselves as financial agents. They feel embarrassed to be a part of this industry. They are not comfortable to be introduced as financial advisors and pause before client meetings. They are into this profession just for the heck of it. If you are one amongst this lot, what you need to believe and understand is that no business is big or small. It is all in your mind.

For instance, what is the first thing that comes to your mind when I say Mr Rohit is a tea-seller? Most people might think Mr Rohit is a tea-stall owner. But, in reality, he can be the manufacturer of tea, distributor of tea, or as you thought a tea-stall owner. Also, he can be the owner of a café or a 5-star hotel where tea is one of the items on the menu. In all these cases, the fact that Mr Rohit is a tea-seller remains unchanged. So, it is entirely upon you as to how you perceive your business and make it grow to the best of your ability.

You should look at this as a service to your clients. You have all the reasons to think highly about this profession. You help your clients manage their hard-earned money and earn even more on their surplus funds. Your clients definitely look up to you and trust you; otherwise, this big responsibility of handling finances wouldn't have been given to you in the first place. Also, the financial industry is growing at a much higher pace as compared to several other industries. People are gradually choosing this as their first career option instead of the last as perceived in older days.

Start by accepting the business that you are in. Make this your full-time profession rather than a part-time job. Love your profession. Enjoy it to the core. Then see it grow over and above your expectations. Client calls and meetings will automatically go up when you are passionate about your profession, as it clearly reflects in your personality. This business of ours has a lot of potential, provided you are ready to dedicate yourself to it and reap the profits in return. Have a broad mindset to keep looking for opportunities whenever they crop up. Take pride in your work and see wonders happening.

I am a living example of what I am preaching to you. Everything I have today, my house, my assets and my lifestyle, also the name and fame, are because of my profession. I owe everything to this industry. I love my profession and enjoy every moment of it. I like every aspect of the business and this has made me put in a lot of hard work, and this has done miracles for me over time.

Once you start loving your profession, you begin with investing in your own self. This will come naturally to you. That is when your brain will identify your weak points and make you work on them.

Take one step at a time. Only when you grow first can you help your company grow better. Until you put your heart and soul into your profession, you will not grow and succeed.

"When you learn to love your job and enjoy it too, new opportunities come knocking in."

8.2 LIFE SKILLS: TODAY AND ALWAYS

"Let's stop calling them soft skills. They are real skills and are learnable."

– Unknown

Life skills, according to psychology, are defined as a set of psychosocial competence and personal skills that help people make big decisions carefully, communicate effectively with others, develop coping skills with surrounding circumstance, and manage oneself such that it leads to progress and success. These are the abilities that help you deal well and effectively with the challenges of everyday life.

Any skill that is useful in your life is the life skill you need. Everyone will potentially have a different list of skills they consider most essential in life. Being able to communicate effectively is the most important of all soft skills. Critical to life and work, it may take a lifetime to master this skill. Effective communication skills are much needed in all aspects of life, from professional to personal to social and everything in between.

The ability to communicate information clearly with accuracy is a vital life skill and should not be overlooked.

Even if you lack this skill, it is never too late to start. Work on your communication skills now and see how it improves your quality of life. In our industry, you need communication skills at every step.

Facts tell and stories sell is a widely accepted reality. And only good communication skills make you a great story-teller. To on-board clients, your communication skill needs to be bang on. Negotiating with the company people also requires you to be good at this skill. To train your team members and get work out of them, effective communication goes a long way.

Inspire and influence to leave a lasting impression in the minds of people around you, especially your clients. And this does not need to be done only professionally. How you live your personal life also affects your career to a great extent. When you achieve something in life worth inspiring others, it becomes the talk of the town. People look up to you and start taking you seriously. In my case, this happened after my weight loss journey and also after I quit smoking. Clients wanted to know more about my journey when they had seen me in bad shape in the past. Many clients still ask me to get into the details even though it has now been a few years since I lost 18 kg and later quit smoking. They get inspired by me and also get influenced by my thoughts to a large extent.

Then, talking about the attitude, you need to learn to leave your ego behind when entering the business circuit. Whether it is your clients or your employees, your ego shouldn't come in between your business. If done otherwise, it will only pull down your business.

Information technology (IT) is a critical field in today's times. It is vital in almost every profession. Keep yourself updated to grow with growing needs.

Decision-making skills and problem-solving skills are required too, especially by leaders to understand problems, find solutions to them and then implement them as well. You need to be able to take quick actions when needed and address the problems effectively.

Along with focusing on your life skills, you need to pay attention to your peer group as well. Ours is a B2C model of business. You need to directly be in touch with the clients. And for this you have to be in the limelight or at least visible to your clients. But only being visible is not enough. Being visible and spending time with the right group of people is very important. It is believed that you are an average of five people you spend most time with. Your social circle should include the best businessmen and professionals in your city. You are known by the company you keep. Your identity and stature are directly connected with the circle you move in.

It is also important for you to upgrade your social circle from time to time. As you grow in your business, you also need to keep growing socially and move into groups of people with high stature and identities. Continuing with the same old group might restrict your growth to a great extent.

Belong to a group wherein there are many learned people who will help you gain knowledge and grow. Being the most intelligent person in the group will only bring you compliments and not lead you to enhanced learning. Leaving your old peer group for a new, intelligent and successful social circle is your ladder to growth.

Mukesh Ambani once said, "If your friends aren't discussing success, stocks, entrepreneurship, business, and giving you positive encouragement, you're in the wrong circle." Spend time with people who will help in enhancing your knowledge and help you grow.

"Effective communication skills are much needed in all aspects of life, from professional to personal to social and everything in between."

9. THE BEGINNING

"Every new beginning comes from some other beginning's end."

A lot of entrepreneurs think that their idea is the whole and sole reason for their success. Their ideas will make them rise and prosper. But it is not true in most cases. Business ideas may come easily, but what takes most effort is the implementation. You must be capable enough to execute the ideas and not simply dream about them.

Likewise, reading this book alone is not going to fetch you success. The strategies and ideas that I have advised in this book can only be successful when they are implemented well. That is when your actual journey begins. How well you execute the proposed strategies is what will actually decide your success.

This book will be read by many financial advisors so the strategies discussed here are not unique to you or your company. The uniqueness lies in your execution process. That is what will make the difference between you and other advisors reading this book. This book will definitely lead you to the path of victory but the effort will be completely yours. It is not possible to move mountains in a day and we all know that. But if the strategies mentioned here are executed step by step, within a span of few years you will be able to reach the pinnacle of success.

To do something new, you have to let go of something old. You have to trade off your old strategies for the new ones mentioned in the book. Only when you decide on quitting your earlier ways will you be able to find time and resources for the newer, better ways.

Read the book carefully and analyse what works for you and what doesn't. You might not be able to apply everything at once. Plan well and then choose your road ahead. Stick to your plan and witness miracles happening day after day. Carry out each and everything mentioned in this book and eventually be sure to establish yourself as a successful financial advisor.

Do not consider this as the end of the book. Look at it as the beginning of a new journey. The journey that will eventually lead to your success.

"Only when you decide on quitting your earlier ways will you be able to find time and resources for the newer, better ways."

ONE IMPORTANT THING...

It would be great to know all the amazing success stories that come to life after you have applied my suggested strategies in your business and personality on the whole. Please send me your feedback on the same. I will make sure to read each of your emails and reply to them personally. Nothing is more rewarding than a reader's email and what could make me happier than hearing about your success after implementing my suggested ideas.

Best wishes
Garvit Chaharia
garvit@deevaventures.com